What Can the Bible Teach Us?

THIS BOOK IS THE PROPERTY OF

_____

Photo Credits:
■ Page 25: WHO photo by Edouard Boubat
■ Pages 96-97: Explosion: Based on USAF photo; child: Based on WHO photo by W. Cutting

Unless otherwise indicated, Scripture quotations are from the modern-language *New World Translation of the Holy Scriptures*.

What Can the Bible Teach Us?
June 2016 Printing
English (*bhs*-E)
© 2015
Watch Tower Bible and Tract Society of Pennsylvania

PUBLISHERS
Watchtower Bible and Tract Society of New York, Inc.
Wallkill, New York, U.S.A.

Made in the United States of America

D1431806

CONTENTS

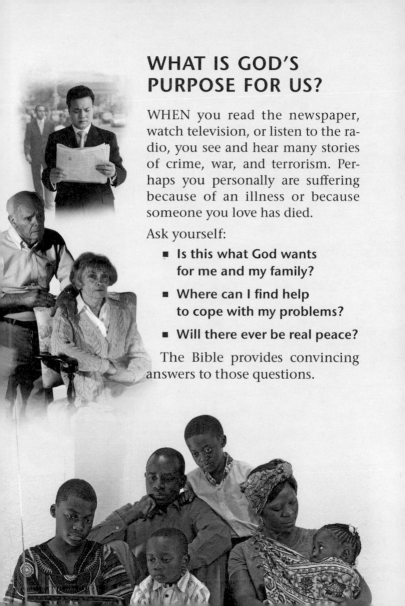

WHAT IS GOD'S PURPOSE FOR US?

WHEN you read the newspaper, watch television, or listen to the radio, you see and hear many stories of crime, war, and terrorism. Perhaps you personally are suffering because of an illness or because someone you love has died.

Ask yourself:

- **Is this what God wants for me and my family?**

- **Where can I find help to cope with my problems?**

- **Will there ever be real peace?**

The Bible provides convincing answers to those questions.

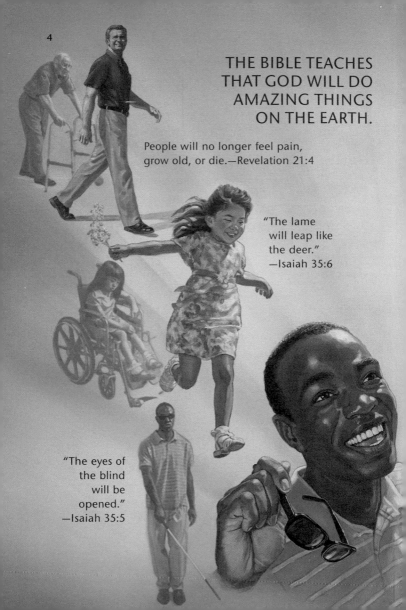

4

THE BIBLE TEACHES THAT GOD WILL DO AMAZING THINGS ON THE EARTH.

People will no longer feel pain, grow old, or die.—Revelation 21:4

"The lame will leap like the deer." —Isaiah 35:6

"The eyes of the blind will be opened." —Isaiah 35:5

The dead will be
brought back to life.
—John 5:28, 29

No one
will get sick.
—Isaiah 33:24

Everyone on earth will
have plenty to eat.
—Psalm 72:16

BENEFIT FROM WHAT THE BIBLE TEACHES

It would be easy to think that what you have read in the first few pages of this book is just a dream. But God has promised to make those changes on the earth very soon, and the Bible explains how he will do so.

The Bible does more than that. It tells us what we need to know in order to be truly happy and enjoy life right now. Think for a moment about the things that make you worry. These may include money or family matters, bad health, or the death of someone you love. The Bible can help you to cope with these problems, and it can comfort you by answering such questions as these:

- Why do we suffer?

- How can we cope with our problems?

- Can our family be happy?

- What happens to us when we die?

- Will we ever see our dead loved ones again?

- Why can we be confident that God will do everything that he has promised?

The fact that you are reading this book shows that you want to know what the Bible teaches. This book will help you. There are questions for the paragraphs, which will help you understand the Bible better. Millions of people have enjoyed discussing the Bible with Jehovah's Witnesses. We hope you will too. May God bless you as you discover what the Bible can teach you!

GET TO KNOW YOUR BIBLE

THE Bible contains 66 books and letters. Each one is divided into chapters and verses. This makes it easy to find a verse. When this publication cites a scripture, the first number after the name of the Bible book indicates the chapter, and the following number refers to the verse. For example, if you see "2 Timothy 3:16," it means the second letter to Timothy, chapter 3, verse 16.

When you look up the scriptures cited, you will quickly become familiar with the Bible. You could also start reading the Bible each day. If you read three to five chapters a day, you can read the entire Bible in a year.

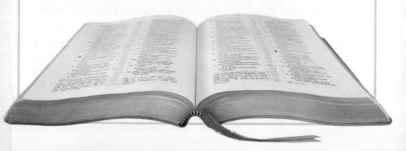

CHAPTER ONE

WHO IS GOD?

CHILDREN ask lots of questions. You may explain something to them, but they often ask, 'Why?' And when you try to give them an answer, they may ask, 'But why?'

² Whether we are young or old, we all have questions. We may have questions about what we will eat or wear or buy. Or we may have important questions about life and the future. But when we don't find satisfying answers to these questions, we may stop looking for answers.

³ Does the Bible have the answers to the important questions we ask? Some people may think so, but they feel that the Bible is too hard to understand. They may think that only teachers or priests have the answers. And others are too ashamed to admit that they don't know the answers. What do you think?

⁴ You probably want answers to questions, such as: Why am I here? What will happen to me when I die? What is God like? Jesus, the famous Teacher, said: "Keep on asking, and it will be given you; keep on seeking, and you will find; keep on knocking, and it

---

1, 2. What questions do people often ask?

3. Why do many people think they can't find the answers to their important questions?

4, 5. What important questions do you have? Why should you keep looking for the answers?

will be opened to you." (Matthew 7:7) Don't give up until you find answers that you can trust.

⁵ Yes, if you "keep on seeking," you will find the answers in the Bible. (Proverbs 2:1-5) These answers are not too hard to understand. What you learn will give you a happier life right now and a wonderful hope for the future. Let's talk about one question that has confused many people.

DOES GOD CARE ABOUT US OR IS HE CRUEL?

⁶ Many people think that God doesn't care about us. They feel that if God really cared, the world would be very different. We see war, hatred, and misery everywhere. People get sick, they suffer, and they die. Some wonder, 'If God cares about us, why doesn't he stop all this suffering?'

⁷ Religious leaders sometimes make people believe that God is cruel. When something terrible happens, they say that it's God's will. They say that he wanted it to happen. When they say this, they are really blaming God. But the Bible teaches that God is **never the source of evil.** James 1:13 tells us that God does not test anyone with evil things. It says: "When under trial, let no one say: 'I am being tried [or, tested] by God.' For with evil things God cannot be tried, nor does he himself try anyone." This means that even though God **hasn't stopped** bad things from

---

6. Why do some people think that God doesn't care about their suffering?

7. (a) How have religious leaders taught people that God is cruel? (b) Why can we be sure that God is not to blame for bad things that happen?

happening, he **never makes** them happen. **(Read Job 34:10-12.)** Let's use an example.

8 Imagine a young man who lives at home with his parents. His father loves him very much and has taught him how to make good decisions. Then, the young man rebels against his father and leaves home. He does bad things and gets into trouble. Would you blame the father for what happened because he didn't stop his son from leaving home? Of course not! (Luke 15:11-13) Like that father, God didn't stop humans when they chose to rebel and do what is bad. So when something bad happens, we should remember that God didn't make it happen. It would be unfair to blame God.

9 There is a very good reason why God has not yet stopped bad things from happening. In Chapter 11, you will learn what the Bible says about this. But you can be sure that God loves us and that he is never to blame for our problems. In fact, he is the only One who can solve them.—Isaiah 33:2.

10 God is holy. (Isaiah 6:3) Everything he does is pure, clean, and good. So we can trust him. Humans are not like that. They sometimes do wrong things. And even the most honest ruler does not have the power to repair all the damage that bad people do. No one has as much power as God has. He can and will repair all the damage that has been done by bad

8, 9. Why would it be unfair to blame God for our problems? Give an example.
10. Why can we be sure that God will repair all the damage that has been done by bad people?

people. He will remove all evil forever.—**Read Psalm 37:9-11.**

HOW DOES GOD FEEL WHEN PEOPLE SUFFER?

11 How does God feel when he sees what is happening in the world and what you are going through? The Bible teaches that God "loves justice." (Psalm 37:28) So he cares deeply about what is right and what is wrong. He hates it when people suffer. The Bible says that "his heart was saddened" when he saw the world filled with badness in the past. (Genesis 6:5, 6) God has not changed. (Malachi 3:6) The Bible says that God really cares about you.—**Read 1 Peter 5:7.**

12 The Bible also says that God created us in his image. (Genesis 1:26) This means that God made us with the same good qualities that he has. So if you feel bad when you see innocent people suffer, God must feel even worse when he sees it! How do we know this?

13 The Bible teaches us that "God is love." (1 John 4:8) Everything God does is motivated by love. So we love because God loves. Think about this: If you had the power, would you remove all the suffering and injustice in the world? Of course you would, because you love people. What about God? He has the power, and because he loves us, he will remove all suffering

---

11. How does God feel about your suffering?
12, 13. (a) Why do we love and care for others, and how do we feel about the suffering in the world? (b) Why can we be sure that God will remove all suffering and injustice?

and injustice. You can be sure that every one of God's promises mentioned at the beginning of this book will come true! But to be able to trust these promises, you need to know more about God.

GOD WANTS YOU TO KNOW HIM

14 If you want to be someone's friend, what's the first thing you usually tell him? Your name. Does God have a name? Many religions say his name is God or Lord, but these are not names. They are just titles, like "king" or "president." God has told us that his name is Jehovah. Psalm 83:18 says: "May people know that you, whose name is Jehovah, you alone are the Most High over all the earth." Bible writers used God's name thousands of times. Jehovah wants you to know his name and to use it. He tells you his name so that you can become his friend.

15 God's name, Jehovah, has deep meaning. It means that God can fulfill any promise he makes and can accomplish his purpose.

If you want to be someone's friend, you tell him your name. God tells us his name in the Bible

14. What is God's name, and how do we know that we should use it?
15. What does the name Jehovah mean?

The Bible teaches that Jehovah is the loving Creator of the universe

Nothing can stop him. Only Jehovah can have this name.*

16 As we read earlier, Psalm 83:18 says about Jehovah: "You **alone** are the Most High." Also, Revelation 15:3 says: "Great and wonderful are your works,

---

* If your Bible does not have the name Jehovah or if you would like more information about the meaning and the pronunciation of God's name, please see Endnote 1.

16, 17. What is the meaning of (a) "the Almighty"? (b) "King of eternity"? (c) "Creator"?

Jehovah God, the Almighty. Righteous and true are your ways, King of eternity." What does the title "the Almighty" mean? It means that Jehovah is more powerful than anyone else in the universe. And the title "King of eternity" means that he has always existed. Psalm 90:2 explains that he is from eternity to eternity. Isn't that amazing!

17 Only Jehovah is the Creator. Revelation 4:11 says: "You are worthy, Jehovah our God, to receive the glory and the honor and the power, because you created all things, and because of your will they came into existence and were created." Yes, from the angels in heaven to the stars in the sky to the fruit on the trees and to the fish in the sea—Jehovah made everything you can think of!

A father loves his children, but our heavenly Father loves us even more

CAN YOU BE JEHOVAH'S FRIEND?

18 When some people read about Jehovah's impressive qualities, they feel afraid and think, 'God is so powerful, so important, and so far away, why would he care about me?' But is that how God wants us to feel? Not at all. Jehovah wants to be close to us. The Bible says that God is "not far off from each one of us." (Acts 17:27) God wants you to draw close to him, and he promises that "he will draw close to you."—James 4:8.

19 How can you become God's friend? Jesus said: "This means everlasting life, their coming to know you, the only true God, and the one whom you sent, Jesus Christ." (John 17:3) Keep on learning, and you will come to know Jehovah and Jesus. And then you can have everlasting life. For example, we have already learned that "God is love." (1 John 4:16) But he also has many other beautiful qualities. The Bible tells us that Jehovah is "merciful and compassionate, slow to anger and abundant in loyal love and truth." (Exodus 34:6) Jehovah is "good and ready to forgive." (Psalm 86:5) God is patient and loyal. (2 Peter 3:9; Revelation 15:4) You will learn much more about his beautiful qualities as you read about him in the Bible.

20 How can you feel close to God if you cannot see

---

18. Why might some people think that they can never be God's friend? What does the Bible say about that?

19. (a) How can you become God's friend? (b) Which of Jehovah's qualities do you like the most?

20-22. (a) How can we feel close to God if we cannot see him? (b) What should you do if others want you to stop studying the Bible?

him? (John 1:18; 4:24; 1 Timothy 1:17) When you read about Jehovah in the Bible, you get to know him as a real Person. (Psalm 27:4; Romans 1:20) As you learn more about Jehovah, you will love him more and more and you will feel closer to him.

²¹ You will understand that Jehovah is our Father. (Matthew 6:9) He gave us life, and he also wants us to have the best life possible. That is what a loving father would want for his children. (Psalm 36:9) Yes, the Bible teaches that you can become Jehovah's friend. (James 2:23) Imagine that. Jehovah, the Creator of the universe, wants you to be his friend!

²² Some people may want you to stop studying the Bible. They may fear that you will change your religion. But don't let anyone stop you from becoming Jehovah's friend. He is the best Friend you could ever have.

²³ As you study the Bible, there will be things that you don't understand. Don't be ashamed to ask questions or to ask for help. Jesus said that we should be humble, like little children. (Matthew 18:2-4) And children ask lots of questions. God wants you to find the answers. So study the Bible carefully to make sure that what you learn is the truth.—**Read Acts 17:11.**

²⁴ The best way to learn about Jehovah is to study the Bible. In the next chapter, we will find out why the Bible is different from every other book.

23, 24. (a) Why should you keep asking questions? (b) What will we discuss in the next chapter?

TRUTH 1 — WHO IS GOD?

"You created all things."—Revelation 4:11

What can the Bible teach us about God?

Revelation 15:3
He is the Almighty,
the most powerful person
in the universe.

Psalm 90:2
He has always existed.

Matthew 6:9
God is our Father.
He wants us to have
the best life possible.

Acts 17:27
God wants to be close to us.

TRUTH 2 — GOD HAS A NAME

"Jehovah . . . is my name forever."—Exodus 3:15

Why is God's name important?

Psalm 83:18
God tells us that his name
is Jehovah. "God" and "Lord"
are not names. They are titles,
like "king" and "president."
Jehovah wants you to use
his name.

Exodus 3:14
His name means
"He Causes to Become."
Because Jehovah created
all things, he can fulfill any
promise he makes and can
accomplish his purpose.

TRUTH 3   JEHOVAH LOVES US

"God is love."—1 John 4:8

What does God's love mean for us?

Exodus 34:6; Psalm 37:28
He is merciful and
compassionate. He
loves truth and justice.

Psalm 86:5
He is forgiving.

2 Peter 3:9
He is patient with us.

Revelation 15:4
He is loyal to us.

TRUTH 4   GOD CARES FOR YOU

"Throw all your anxiety on him,
because he cares for you."—1 Peter 5:7

How do you know that God really cares for you?

Psalm 37:9-11
He promises to end suffering
and to repair all the damage
done by bad people.

James 4:8
Jehovah wants you
to be close to him.

John 17:3
The more you learn about
God, the more you will
love him.

CHAPTER TWO

THE BIBLE
—A BOOK FROM GOD

HOW do you feel when a friend surprises you with a gift? You can't wait to open it, and you are happy that your friend thought of you. You thank him for it.

² The Bible is a gift from God. It gives us information that we can't find anywhere else. For example, it tells us that God created the heavens, the earth, and the first man and woman. It gives us principles that can help us when we have problems. In the Bible, we learn how God will accomplish his purpose to make the earth a better place. The Bible is such an exciting gift!

³ As you study the Bible, you will discover that God wants you to be his friend. The more you learn about him, the closer your friendship with him will become.

⁴ The Bible has been translated into about 2,600 languages, and billions of copies have been printed. More than 90 percent of the people in the world can read the Bible in their own language. And **each week**, more than a million people get a Bible! Yes, there is no other book like the Bible.

1, 2. Why is the Bible an exciting gift from God?
3. What will you learn as you study the Bible?
4. What impresses you about the Bible?

The *New World Translation of the Holy Scriptures* is available in many languages

5 The Bible is "inspired of God." **(Read 2 Timothy 3:16.)** But some may think, 'The Bible was written by men, so how can it be from God?' The Bible answers: "Men spoke from God as they were moved [or, guided] by holy spirit." (2 Peter 1:21) This is similar to a businessman telling his secretary to write a letter. Who is the author of the letter? It is the businessman, not the secretary. In the same way, the Author of the Bible is God, not the men he used to write it. God guided them to write his thoughts. The Bible really is "the word of God."—1 Thessalonians 2:13; see Endnote 2.

5. Why can we say that the Bible is "inspired of God"?

THE BIBLE IS ACCURATE

6 It took more than 1,600 years to write the Bible. Its writers lived at different times. Some were well-educated and others were not. For example, one was a doctor. Others were farmers, fishermen, shepherds, prophets, judges, and kings. Even though there were different writers, all parts of the Bible agree. It doesn't say one thing in one chapter and the opposite in another.*

7 The first chapters of the Bible explain how the world's problems started, and the last chapters tell us how God will solve those problems by making the earth a paradise. The Bible covers thousands of years of human history and shows that God's purpose is always accomplished.

8 The Bible wasn't written to teach science or to be a school textbook, but what it says about scientific matters is always accurate. That is what we would expect of a book that comes from God. For example, the book of Leviticus contains God's instructions on ways the Israelites could stop disease from spreading. This was written long before people knew how bacteria and viruses cause disease. The Bible also correctly teaches that the earth hangs on nothing. (Job 26:7) And when most people believed that the earth

---

* Some people say that the Bible is not harmonious, but that is not true. See chapter 7 of the book *The Bible—God's Word or Man's?* published by Jehovah's Witnesses.

6, 7. Why can we say that the Bible is harmonious?
8. Give examples that show the scientific accuracy of the Bible.

was flat, the Bible said that it was round.—Isaiah 40:22.

⁹ When the Bible talks about history, it is always accurate. But many history books are not completely accurate because the writers were not honest. For example, they did not always write about the times their nation was defeated in battle. Instead, Bible writers were honest even when Israel was defeated. They also wrote about their own mistakes. For example, in the book of Numbers, Moses tells us that he made a serious mistake and that God had to discipline him for it. (Numbers 20:2-12) The honesty of Bible writers shows that the Bible comes from God. This means that we can trust the Bible.

A BOOK FULL OF GOOD ADVICE

¹⁰ The Bible is "inspired of God and beneficial for teaching, for reproving, for setting things straight." (2 Timothy 3:16) Yes, the Bible's advice is helpful for us today. Jehovah knows how we are made, so he understands how we think and feel. He knows us better than we know ourselves, and he wants us to be happy. He knows what is good for us and what is bad for us.

¹¹ In Matthew chapters 5 to 7, we read very good advice that Jesus gave on how to be happy, how to get along with others, how to pray, and how to view

---

9. What does the honesty of the Bible writers help us to understand?

10. Why is the Bible's advice helpful for us today?

11, 12. (a) What good advice did Jesus give in Matthew chapters 5 to 7? (b) What else can we learn from the Bible?

money. Although he gave this advice 2,000 years ago, it is just as powerful and helpful today.

¹² In the Bible, Jehovah also teaches us principles that help us to have a better family life, to be good workers, and to live in peace with others. Bible principles can always help us, no matter who we are, where we live, or what problems we have.—**Read Isaiah 48:17;** see Endnote 3.

YOU CAN TRUST BIBLE PROPHECY

¹³ Many Bible prophecies have already come true. For example, Isaiah prophesied that Babylon would be destroyed. (Isaiah 13:19) He described exactly how the city would be defeated. The city was protected by large gates and a river. But Isaiah foretold that the river would be dried up and the gates left open. The attackers would take the city without a battle. Isaiah even prophesied that a man named Cyrus would defeat Babylon.—**Read Isaiah 44:27–45:2;** see Endnote 4.

¹⁴ Two hundred years after the prophecy was written, an army arrived ready to attack Babylon. Who was leading the army? Just as the prophecy said, it was Cyrus, the king of Persia. Everything was set for the rest of the prophecy to come true.

¹⁵ On the night of the attack, the Babylonians were having a feast. They felt safe because they were protected by massive walls and a river. Outside the

---

13. What did Isaiah say would happen to the city of Babylon?
14, 15. How did Isaiah's prophecy come true?

The Bible writer Isaiah foretold that Babylon would be defeated

city, Cyrus and his army dug a channel to lower the level of the river water. The water level went down enough for the Persian soldiers to walk through it. But how would the army get past Babylon's walls? Just as the prophecy said, the city gates were left open, so the soldiers took the city without a battle.

16 Isaiah prophesied that eventually no one would ever live in Babylon again. He wrote: "She will never be inhabited, nor will she be a place to reside [or, live] in throughout all generations." (Isaiah 13:20) Did that come true? In the place where Babylon used to be, about 50 miles south of Baghdad, Iraq, there are just ruins. Even today, no one lives there. Jehovah swept Babylon "with the broom of annihilation [or, destruction]."—Isaiah 14:22, 23.*

17 The fact that so many Bible prophecies have already come true means that we can trust what the Bible says about the future. We can be sure that

---

* If you would like to learn more about Bible prophecy, you can read pages 27-29 of the brochure *A Book for All People,* published by Jehovah's Witnesses.

---

16. (a) What did Isaiah prophesy about the future of Babylon? (b) How do we know that Isaiah's prophecy came true?
17. Why can we trust all of God's promises?

The ruins of Babylon

Jehovah will keep his promise to make the earth a paradise. **(Read Numbers 23:19.)** Yes, we have the hope of "everlasting life that God, who cannot lie, promised long ago."—Titus 1:2.*

THE BIBLE CAN CHANGE YOUR LIFE

18 We have learned that there is no other book like the Bible. It is harmonious, and when it talks about scientific or historical matters, it is always accurate. It also gives us good advice and contains many prophecies that have already come true. But the Bible does even more than that. The apostle Paul wrote: "The word of God is alive and exerts power." What does that mean?—**Read Hebrews 4:12.**

19 The Bible can change your life. It can help you to know who you really are. It can help you to understand your deepest thoughts and feelings. For example, we may think that we love God. But to prove that we love him, we need to apply what the Bible says.

20 The Bible truly is a book from God. He wants you to read it, study it, and love it. Be thankful for this gift, and keep studying it. Then you will understand God's purpose for humans. In the next chapter, we will learn more about this purpose.

---

* The destruction of Babylon is just one Bible prophecy that came true. You can find information on prophecies about Jesus Christ in Endnote 5.

---

18. How does Paul describe "the word of God"?
19, 20. (a) How can the Bible help you to know who you are? (b) How can you show that you are thankful for the gift of the Bible?

TRUTH 1   THE BIBLE IS FROM GOD

"All Scripture is inspired of God."—2 Timothy 3:16

How is the Bible different from any other book?

The Bible has been translated into about 2,600 languages, and billions of copies have been printed.

It gives us information that we cannot find anywhere else.

1 Thessalonians 2:13
The Author of the Bible is God.

2 Peter 1:21
God guided men to express his thoughts.

TRUTH 2   THE BIBLE IS A BOOK OF PROPHECY

"God . . . cannot lie."—Titus 1:2

Why can you trust the Bible?

Isaiah 44:27–45:2
Hundreds of years before it happened, the Bible prophesied how Babylon would be conquered.

2 Timothy 3:1-5
Bible prophecies are being fulfilled now.

Numbers 23:19
We can trust what the Bible says about the future.

TRUTH 3 — THE BIBLE IS DESIGNED TO HELP YOU

"I, Jehovah, am your God, the One teaching you to benefit yourself."—Isaiah 48:17

What have you learned about the Bible?

Job 26:7; Isaiah 40:22
What the Bible says about scientific matters is accurate.

Numbers 20:2-12
Bible writers were honest.

Matthew 5-7
Jesus gave us advice on how to be happy, how to get along with others, how to pray, and how to view money.

TRUTH 4 — THE BIBLE CAN CHANGE YOUR LIFE

"The word of God is alive and exerts power."
—Hebrews 4:12

What can God's Word do for you?

- It can help you to understand God's purpose.
- It can help you to know what kind of person you are.
- It can help you to understand what God expects of you.

God wants you to read, study, and love the Bible.

CHAPTER THREE

WHAT IS GOD'S PURPOSE FOR HUMANS?

GOD has a wonderful purpose for humans. He created the first man and woman, Adam and Eve, to live in a beautiful garden. His purpose was for them to have children, to make the whole earth a paradise, and to take care of the animals.—Genesis 1:28; 2:8, 9, 15; see Endnote 6.

2 Do you think that we will ever live in a paradise? Jehovah tells us: "I have purposed it, and I will also carry it out." (Isaiah 46:9-11; 55:11) Yes, he will do what he has purposed, and nothing will stop him. Jehovah says that he created the earth for a reason. He "did not create it simply for nothing." (Isaiah 45:18) He wants people to live all over the earth. What kind of people does God want to live here, and for how long? The Bible says: "The **righteous** [or, obedient] will possess the earth, and they will **live forever** on it."—Psalm 37:29; Revelation 21:3, 4.

3 But today people get sick and die. In many places, they fight and kill one another. Surely this is not what God purposed. So, what happened, and why? Only the Bible can explain.

---

1. What is God's purpose for humans?
2. (a) How do we know that God will do what he has purposed? (b) What does the Bible say about living forever?
3. Since humans get sick and die, what might you ask?

AN ENEMY OF GOD

4 The Bible tells us that God has an enemy who is "called Devil and Satan." Satan used a snake to speak to Eve in the garden of Eden. (Revelation 12:9; Genesis 3:1) He made it look as though the snake was talking.—See Endnote 7.

5 So, did God create Satan the Devil? No! **An angel** who had been in heaven when God prepared the earth for Adam and Eve **changed and became the Devil.** (Job 38:4, 7) How was that possible? Well, how does an honest person change and become a thief? He was not born a thief. But he desires, or wants, something that doesn't belong to him. He **keeps thinking about it**, and his wrong desire becomes stronger. Then, when he gets a chance, he steals it. He has turned himself into a thief.—**Read James 1:13-15;** see Endnote 8.

6 This is what happened to that angel. After Jehovah created Adam and Eve, he told them to have children and "fill the earth." (Genesis 1:27, 28) That angel may have thought, 'All those people could worship me instead of Jehovah!' The more he thought about it, the more he desired what belongs to Jehovah. That angel wanted people to worship him. So he lied to Eve and misled her. **(Read Genesis 3:1-5.)** By doing that, he became Satan the Devil, an enemy of God.

7 Adam and Eve disobeyed God and ate the fruit.

4, 5. (a) Who spoke to Eve through a snake in the garden of Eden? (b) How can a person who is honest become a thief?
6. How did an angel become an enemy of God?
7. (a) Why did Adam and Eve die? (b) Why do we grow old and die?

(Genesis 2:17; 3:6) They sinned against Jehovah, and in time they died, just as Jehovah had said they would. (Genesis 3:17-19) Adam and Eve's children were sinners, so they died. **(Read Romans 5:12.)** To help us understand why Adam and Eve's children were also sinners, consider this example. Imagine baking a loaf of bread in a pan that has a dent. The bread will have the same dent as the pan. When Adam disobeyed God, Adam became a sinner. Because we are Adam's children, all of us are sinners, or have the same "dent" as he did. And because we are all sinners, we grow old and die.—Romans 3:23; see Endnote 9.

8 Satan started a rebellion against Jehovah when he influenced Adam and Eve to disobey God. He wanted Adam and Eve to believe that Jehovah is a liar, a bad ruler who didn't want the best for them. Satan was saying that humans don't need God to tell them what to do and that Adam and Eve should decide for themselves what was right and wrong. So, what would Jehovah do? He could have killed the rebels and ended the rebellion. But would that have proved that Satan is a liar? No, it wouldn't.

9 Thus, Jehovah didn't kill the rebels immediately. Instead, he allowed time for humans to rule themselves. This would make it clear that Satan is a liar and that Jehovah knows what is best for humans. We will learn more about that in Chapter 11. But what do you think about Adam and Eve's decision? Was

---

8, 9. (a) What did Satan want Adam and Eve to believe? (b) Why did Jehovah not kill the rebels immediately?

it right for them to believe Satan and disobey God? Jehovah had given Adam and Eve everything they had. He gave them perfect life, a beautiful place to live, and work that they enjoyed. But Satan had never done anything good for them. If you had been there, what would you have done?

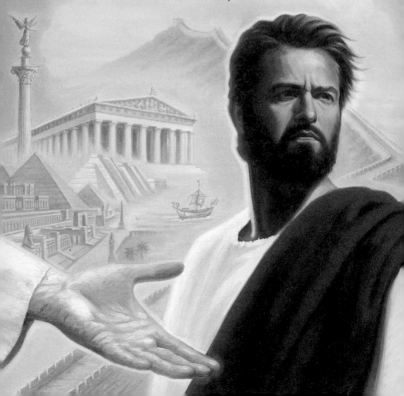

If all the kingdoms of the world didn't belong to Satan, could he have offered them to Jesus?

10 Today, each of us has a similar choice to make, and our life depends on that choice. We can choose to obey Jehovah as our Ruler and help prove that Satan is a liar. Or we can choose Satan as our ruler. (Psalm 73:28; **read Proverbs 27:11**.) Very few people in this world obey God. In fact, he is not the ruler of the world. But if God isn't, who is?

WHO RULES THE WORLD?

11 Jesus knew who really rules the world. On one occasion, Satan "showed him all the kingdoms of the world and their glory." Then Satan promised Jesus: "All these things I will give you if you fall [or, bow] down and do an act of worship to me." (Matthew 4: 8, 9; Luke 4:5, 6) Ask yourself, 'If those kingdoms didn't belong to Satan, could he have offered them to Jesus?' No. All governments belong to Satan.

12 You may wonder: 'How could Satan be the ruler of the world? Isn't Jehovah the Almighty God who created the universe?' (Revelation 4:11) Yes, he is, but Jesus clearly called Satan "the ruler of this world." (John 12:31; 14:30; 16:11) The apostle Paul called Satan the Devil "the god of this system of things." (2 Corinthians 4:3, 4) And the apostle John wrote that "the whole world is lying in the power of the wicked one."—1 John 5:19.

HOW WILL SATAN'S WORLD BE DESTROYED?

13 This world is becoming more and more

10. What important choice does each of us have?
11, 12. (a) What do we learn from Satan's offer to Jesus? (b) What scriptures show that Satan rules the world?
13. Why do we need a new world?

dangerous. We see wars, corruption, hypocrisy, and violence all around us. Humans cannot get rid of all these problems, no matter how hard they try. But God will soon destroy this wicked world during his war of Armageddon, and he will replace it with a righteous new world.—Revelation 16:14-16; see Endnote 10.

14 Jehovah chose Jesus Christ to be the King of His heavenly government, or Kingdom. Thousands of years ago, the Bible foretold that Jesus would rule as "Prince of Peace" and that his government would never end. (Isaiah 9:6, 7) Jesus taught his followers to pray for this government when he said: "Let your Kingdom come. Let your will take place, as in heaven, also on earth." (Matthew 6:10) In Chapter 8, we will learn how God's Kingdom will replace the world's governments. **(Read Daniel 2:44.)** Then God's Kingdom will make the earth into a beautiful paradise.—See Endnote 11.

A NEW WORLD IS NEAR!

15 The Bible promises: "There are new heavens and a new earth that we are awaiting," and "in these righteousness is to dwell." (2 Peter 3:13; Isaiah 65:17) Sometimes when the Bible talks about "the earth," it's talking about the people who live on the earth. (Genesis 11:1) So the righteous "new earth" refers to all the people who obey God and are blessed by him.

---

14. Whom has God chosen to be King of His Kingdom? What did the Bible foretell about Jesus?
15. What is the "new earth"?

16 Jesus promised that those who live in God's new world will be given "everlasting life." (Mark 10:30) What must we do to receive this gift? Please **read John 3:16 and 17:3** to find the answer. Let us now see what the Bible says life will be like in the earthly Paradise.

17 **Wickedness, war, crime, and violence will be gone.** There will not be any wicked people left on earth. (Psalm 37:10, 11) God will bring "an end to wars throughout the earth." (Psalm 46:9; Isaiah 2:4) The earth will be full of people who love God and are obedient to him. There will be peace forever.—Psalm 72:7.

18 **Jehovah's people will feel secure.** In Bible times, when the Israelites obeyed God, they were safe because he protected them. (Leviticus 25:18, 19) In the Paradise, we will not be afraid of anything or anybody. We will always feel secure!—**Read Isaiah 32:18; Micah 4:4.**

19 **There will be plenty of food.** "There will be an abundance of grain on the earth; on the top of the mountains it will overflow." (Psalm 72:16) Jehovah, "our God, will bless us," and "the earth will give its produce."—Psalm 67:6.

20 **The whole earth will become a paradise.** People will have beautiful houses and gardens. **(Read Isaiah**

---

16. What wonderful gift will God give to those who live in his new world, and what must we do to receive this gift?
17, 18. How do we know that there will be peace everywhere on the earth and that we will feel secure?
19. Why can we be sure that there will be plenty of food in God's new world?
20. How do we know that the earth will become a paradise?

65:21-24; Revelation 11:18.) The whole earth will be as beautiful as the garden of Eden was. Jehovah will always give us everything that we need. The Bible says about him: "You open your hand and satisfy the desire of every living thing."—Psalm 145:16.

21 There will be peace between humans and animals. Animals will not harm humans anymore. Little children will feel safe, even around animals that are dangerous to us today.—**Read Isaiah 11:6-9; 65:25.**

22 No one will be sick. When Jesus was on earth, he healed many people. (Matthew 9:35; Mark 1:40-42; John 5:5-9) But as King of God's Kingdom, Jesus will heal everyone. No one will ever say: "I am sick." —Isaiah 33:24; 35:5, 6.

23 The dead will live again. God promises that he will resurrect millions of people who have died. "There is going to be a resurrection of both the righteous and the unrighteous."—**Read John 5:28, 29;** Acts 24:15.

24 We all have a choice. We can choose to learn about Jehovah and serve him, or we can just do what we want to do. If we choose to serve Jehovah, we can have a wonderful future. When a man asked Jesus to remember him after he died, Jesus promised him: "You will be with me in Paradise." (Luke 23:43) Let us learn more about Jesus Christ and how he will make God's wonderful promises come true.

---

21. How do we know that there will be peace between humans and animals?
22. What will Jesus do for those who are sick?
23. What will God do for those who have died?
24. How do you feel about living in Paradise?

TRUTH 1   GOD CREATED US FOR A PURPOSE

"The righteous will possess the earth, and they will live forever on it."—Psalm 37:29

What is God's purpose for humans?

Genesis 1:28
God wanted families to make the earth a paradise and to look after the animals.

Isaiah 46:9-11; 55:11
God will do what he has purposed, and nothing will stop him.

TRUTH 2   WHY LIFE IS DIFFICULT

"The whole world is lying in the power of the wicked one."—1 John 5:19

Who rules the world?

John 12:31
Jesus called Satan the ruler of the world.

James 1:13-15
Satan wanted what did not belong to him.

Genesis 2:17; 3:1-6
Satan misled Eve, Adam and Eve disobeyed God, and later Adam and Eve both died.

Romans 3:23; 5:12
We die because we inherited sin from Adam.

2 Corinthians 4:3, 4
Satan misleads people.

TRUTH 3

GOD'S KINGDOM WILL SOLVE THE PROBLEM

"Let your Kingdom come. Let your will take place . . . on earth."—Matthew 6:10

What will Jehovah do?

Daniel 2:44
God's government will replace all the world's governments.

Revelation 16:14-16
God will destroy this wicked world at Armageddon.

Isaiah 9:6, 7
Jehovah has chosen Jesus to be the King of His heavenly government. Jesus will rule over the earth.

TRUTH 4

GOD'S KINGDOM WILL MAKE THE EARTH A PARADISE

"You open your hand and satisfy the desire of every living thing."—Psalm 145:16

What will God's Kingdom do for us?

Psalm 46:9
War, crime, and violence will be gone.

Isaiah 32:18; 65:21-24
In the new world, all will have beautiful houses and gardens and will live in peace.

Psalm 72:16
There will be plenty of food.

Isaiah 11:6-9
There will be peace between humans and animals.

Isaiah 33:24; Acts 24:15
No one will be sick, and the dead will live again.

CHAPTER FOUR

WHO IS
JESUS CHRIST?

THERE are many famous people in the world. You may know the name of someone famous. But just because you know his name doesn't mean that you know him well. It doesn't mean that you know every detail about his life and what he is really like.

2 You may have heard about Jesus Christ, even though he lived on earth about 2,000 years ago. But most people do not know what Jesus was like as a person. Some say he was a good man, some say he was a prophet, and some believe that he is God. What do you think?—See Endnote 12.

3 It is important for you to know the truth about Jesus. Why? The Bible tells us: "This means everlasting life, their coming to know you, the only true God, and **the one whom you sent, Jesus Christ.**" (John 17:3) Yes, if you know the truth about Jehovah and Jesus, you can live forever on a paradise earth. (John 14:6) Also, knowing about Jesus will help you because he is the best example of how to live and treat others. (John 13:34, 35) In Chapter 1, we learned the truth about God. Now we will learn what the Bible teaches about Jesus.

1, 2. (a) Do you really know someone famous if you know only his name? Explain. (b) What do people believe about Jesus?
3. Why is it important for you to know Jehovah God and Jesus Christ?

WE HAVE FOUND
THE MESSIAH!

4 Many years before Jesus was born, Jehovah promised in the Bible that he would send the Messiah, or Christ. The word "Messiah" comes from the Hebrew language, and the word "Christ" comes from the Greek. Both of these titles mean that God would choose the promised Messiah and give him a special position. The Messiah will make all of God's promises come true. Jesus can also help you right now. But before Jesus was born, many people wondered, 'Who will be the Messiah?'

5 Jesus' disciples had no doubt that he was the promised Messiah. (John 1:41) For example, Simon Peter said to Jesus: "You are the Christ." (Matthew 16: 16) How can we be sure that Jesus is the Messiah?

6 Long before Jesus was born, God's prophets wrote down many details that would help people find the Messiah. How would this help? Suppose you were asked to go to a busy bus station to pick up a person you had never met. If someone gave you a good description of that person, you would be able to find him. In the same way, Jehovah used his prophets to tell us about what the Messiah would do and what would happen to him. The fulfillment of all those prophecies helps sincere people to know that Jesus is the Messiah.

---

4. What do the words "Messiah" and "Christ" mean?
5. Did Jesus' disciples believe that he was the Messiah?
6. How did Jehovah help sincere people to identify the Messiah?

7 Here are two of those prophecies. First, 700 years before Jesus was born, Micah prophesied that the Messiah would be born in the small town of Bethlehem. (Micah 5:2) And that's where Jesus was born! (Matthew 2:1, 3-9) Second, Daniel prophesied that the Messiah would appear in the year 29 C.E. (Daniel 9:25) These are just two of the many prophecies that clearly prove that Jesus is the promised Messiah.—See Endnote 13.

8 Jehovah has made it very clear that Jesus is the Messiah. God promised to give John the Baptizer a sign so that he would know who the Messiah was. When Jesus went to John to get baptized in the Jordan River in the year 29 C.E., John saw that sign. The Bible tells us what happened: "After being baptized, Jesus immediately came up from the water; and look! the heavens were opened up, and he saw God's spirit descending like a dove and coming upon him. Look! Also, a voice from the heavens said: 'This is my Son, the beloved, whom I have approved.'" (Matthew 3:16, 17) When John saw and heard this sign, he knew that Jesus was the Messiah. (John 1:32-34) On that day, when Jehovah poured out his spirit

---

7. What are two prophecies that prove that Jesus is the Messiah?
8, 9. What happened at Jesus' baptism that proves he is the Messiah?

on him, Jesus became the Messiah. He was the one whom God had chosen to be Leader and King.—Isaiah 55:4.

⁹ Bible prophecies, Jehovah's own words, and the sign He gave at Jesus' baptism prove that Jesus is the Messiah. But where did Jesus come from, and what was he like? Let us see what the Bible says.

At his baptism, Jesus became
the Messiah, or Christ

WHERE DID JESUS COME FROM?

10 The Bible teaches that Jesus lived in heaven for a long time before he came to earth. Micah said that the Messiah was "from ancient times." (Micah 5:2) Jesus himself said many times that he had lived in heaven before being born as a human. **(Read John 3: 13; 6:38, 62; 17:4, 5.)** Even before coming to earth, Jesus had a special relationship with Jehovah.

11 Jesus is very precious to Jehovah. Why? Because God created him before everything and everyone else. So Jesus is called "the firstborn of all creation."* (Colossians 1:15) Jesus is also precious to Jehovah because he is the only one Jehovah created directly. That is why he is called the "only-begotten Son." (John 3:16) Jesus is also the only one Jehovah used to create all other things. (Colossians 1:16) And only Jesus is called "the Word," because Jehovah used him to give messages and instructions to angels and humans.—John 1:14.

12 Some people believe that Jesus and God are the same person. But that's not what the Bible teaches. The Bible says that Jesus was created, which means that Jesus had a beginning. But Jehovah, who created

---

* Jehovah is called a Father because he is the Creator. (Isaiah 64:8) Jesus is called God's Son because Jehovah created him. Angels, as well as the man Adam, are also called sons of God.—Job 1:6; Luke 3:38.

---

10. What does the Bible teach about Jesus' life before he came to earth?
11. Why is Jesus so precious to Jehovah?
12. How do we know that Jesus and God are not the same person?

all things, had no beginning. (Psalm 90:2) As God's Son, Jesus never thought of trying to be God. The Bible clearly teaches that the Father is greater than the Son. **(Read John 14:28;** 1 Corinthians 11:3.) Only Jehovah is "God Almighty." (Genesis 17:1) He is the greatest and most powerful person in the universe. —See Endnote 14.

[13] Jehovah and his Son, Jesus, worked closely together for billions of years before the heavens and the earth were created. They must have loved each other very much! (John 3:35; 14:31) Jesus imitated his father's qualities so well that the Bible calls him "the image of the invisible God."—Colossians 1:15.

[14] Jehovah's precious Son was willing to leave heaven and be born on earth as a human. How was that possible? Jehovah miraculously transferred his Son's life from heaven to the womb of a virgin named Mary. In this way, Jesus did not need to have a human father. So Mary gave birth to a perfect son, and she called him Jesus.—Luke 1:30-35.

WHAT WAS JESUS LIKE?

[15] You can learn a lot about Jesus, his life, and his qualities by reading the Bible books of Matthew, Mark, Luke, and John. Those books are called the Gospels. Because Jesus is just like his Father, what

---

13. Why does the Bible say that Jesus is "the image of the invisible God"?
14. How could Jehovah's precious Son be born as a human?
15. How can you come to know Jehovah better?

you read will also help you come to know Jehovah
better. That is why Jesus could say: "Whoever has
seen me has seen the Father also."—John 14:9.

¹⁶ Many people called Jesus "Teacher." (John 1:38;
13:13) One of the most important things that he
taught was "the good news of the Kingdom." What is
this Kingdom? It is God's government that will rule
over the entire earth from heaven and bring blessings to people who obey God. (Matthew 4:23) Everything Jesus taught came from Jehovah. Jesus said:
"What I teach is not mine, but belongs to him who
sent me." (John 7:16) Jesus knew that Jehovah wants
people to hear the good news that God's Kingdom
will rule over the earth.

¹⁷ Where did Jesus teach? Everywhere he found
people. He taught in the countryside as well as in cities, villages, markets, places of worship, and people's
homes. He didn't expect people to come to him. He
often went to them. (Mark 6:56; Luke 19:5, 6) Jesus
worked hard and spent much time and energy teaching people. Why? Because he knew that God wanted
him to do that and because he always obeyed his
Father. (John 8:28, 29) Jesus also preached because
he felt compassion for people. **(Read Matthew 9:35,
36.)** He could see that the religious leaders were not
teaching the truth about God and his Kingdom. So
he wanted to help as many as possible to hear the
good news.

16. What did Jesus teach? Where did Jesus' teachings come from?
17. Where did Jesus teach? Why did he work so hard to teach others?

[18] Jesus was a man who loved people and cared for them. He was kind and easy to talk to. Even children liked to be with him. (Mark 10:13-16) Jesus was always fair. He hated corruption and injustice. (Matthew 21:12, 13) He lived at a time when women didn't have many rights and were not treated with respect. But Jesus always treated women with respect and dignity. (John 4:9, 27) Jesus was also truly humble. For example, one evening he washed the feet of his apostles, something that was normally done by a servant.—John 13:2-5, 12-17.

[19] Jesus knew what people really needed, and he wanted to help them. This was very clear when he used God's power to heal people miraculously. (Matthew 14:14) For example, a man with leprosy came to Jesus and said: "If you just want to, you can make me clean." Jesus was moved by this man's pain and suffering. He felt sorry for him and wanted to help him. So Jesus stretched out his hand, touched the man, and said to him: "I want to! Be made clean." And the sick man was healed! (Mark 1:40-42) Can you imagine how that man must have felt?

ALWAYS FAITHFUL TO HIS FATHER

[20] Jesus is the best example of obedience to God. No matter what happened or what his enemies did to him, he was faithful to his Father. For example, Jesus did not sin when Satan tried to tempt him.

---

18. What qualities of Jesus do you like the most?
19. What example shows that Jesus knew what people really needed and that he wanted to help them?
20, 21. How is Jesus the best example of obedience to God?

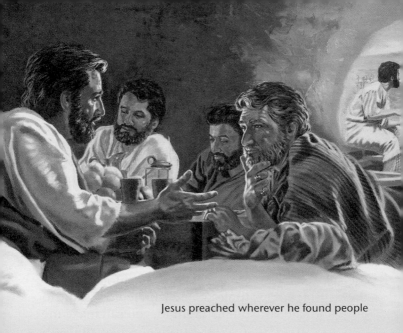

Jesus preached wherever he found people

(Matthew 4:1-11) Some of Jesus' own family didn't believe he was the Messiah and said that he was "out of his mind," but Jesus kept doing God's work. (Mark 3:21) When his enemies were cruel to him, Jesus stayed faithful to God and never tried to harm them. —1 Peter 2:21-23.

²¹ Even when Jesus suffered a cruel and painful death, he stayed faithful to Jehovah. **(Read Philippians 2:8.)** Imagine how much he had to endure on the day he died. He was arrested, false witnesses accused him of blasphemy, corrupt judges condemned him, mobs laughed at him, and soldiers tortured him and nailed him to a stake. When he was dying

he cried out: "It has been accomplished!" (John 19:30) Three days after Jesus died, Jehovah resurrected him and gave him a spirit body. (1 Peter 3:18) A few weeks later, Jesus returned to heaven, "sat down at the right hand of God," and waited for God to make him King.—Hebrews 10:12, 13.

22 Because Jesus remained faithful to his Father, we now have the opportunity to live forever on a paradise earth, just as Jehovah purposed. In the next chapter, we will discuss how Jesus' death makes it possible for us to live forever.

---

22. What opportunity do we now have because Jesus was faithful to his Father?

TRUTH 1   JESUS IS THE MESSIAH

"You are the Christ."—Matthew 16:16

How do we know that Jesus is the Messiah?

**Matthew 3:16, 17;
John 1:32-34**
Jehovah identified Jesus
as his Son.

**Micah 5:2;
Matthew 2:1, 3-9**
Jesus fulfilled all the
prophecies about
the Messiah.

TRUTH 2   JESUS WAS AN ANGEL BEFORE HE CAME TO THE EARTH

"I have come down from heaven."—John 6:38

What did Jesus do in heaven?

Colossians 1:15, 16
Jehovah created Jesus first,
and then he used Jesus
to make all other things.
Jesus learned from his Father
for billions of years.

Luke 1:30-35
Jehovah sent Jesus
to the earth.

TRUTH 3   JESUS LOVES PEOPLE

"Let the young children come to me."—Mark 10:14

What qualities of Jesus do you like?

Mark 10:13-16
Jesus was kind, and people enjoyed talking to him.

John 4:9, 27
Jesus treated women with respect and dignity.

John 13:2-5, 12-17
Jesus was humble.

**Matthew 9:35, 36;
Mark 1:40-42**
Jesus wanted to help others.

TRUTH 4   JESUS ALWAYS DOES GOD'S WILL

"I have . . . finished the work you have given me to do."—John 17:4

How does Jesus' example help us to be faithful?

Matthew 4:1-11
Jesus was faithful when tempted by the Devil.

Mark 3:21
Jesus did God's will even when his relatives mocked him.

1 Peter 2:21-23
Jesus never harmed his enemies.

Philippians 2:8
Jesus stayed faithful to God, even to death.

**Hebrews 10:12, 13;
1 Peter 3:18**
Jehovah resurrected Jesus to heaven.

CHAPTER FIVE

THE RANSOM
—GOD'S GREATEST GIFT

WHAT is the best gift you have ever received? A gift doesn't have to be expensive to be valuable to you. When a gift makes you happy or is something you really need, you feel grateful for it.

² Of all the gifts that God has given us, there is one gift that we need more than anything else. It is God's greatest gift to humans. In this chapter, we will learn that Jehovah sent his Son, Jesus Christ, so that we can live forever. **(Read Matthew 20:28.)** By sending Jesus to the earth as a ransom, Jehovah has proved that he really loves us.

WHAT IS THE RANSOM?

³ The ransom is Jehovah's way of freeing humans from sin and death. (Ephesians 1:7) To understand why the ransom was needed, we have to know what happened thousands of years ago in the garden of Eden. Our first parents, Adam and Eve, sinned. Because they sinned, they died. We also die because we inherited sin from Adam and Eve.—See Endnote 9.

⁴ When Jehovah created the first man, Adam, He

1, 2. (a) What makes a gift valuable to you? (b) Why is the ransom God's greatest gift?
3. Why do humans die?
4. Who was Adam, and what did he have?

gave him something very precious. He gave Adam perfect human life. He had a perfect mind and a perfect body. He would never get sick, would never grow old, and would never die. Because Jehovah created Adam, He was like a father to him. (Luke 3: 38) Jehovah regularly talked to him. God clearly explained to Adam what he expected from him and gave him enjoyable work to do.—Genesis 1:28-30; 2: 16, 17.

[5] Adam was created "in God's image." (Genesis 1: 27) Jehovah gave him qualities like His own, including love, wisdom, justice, and power. He gave Adam free will. Adam was not a robot. God created him so that he could choose to do right or wrong. If Adam had chosen to obey God, he could have lived forever in Paradise.

[6] When he disobeyed God and was sentenced to death, Adam paid a very high price. He lost his special friendship with Jehovah, his perfect life, and his Paradise home. (Genesis 3:17-19) Adam and Eve chose to disobey God, so there was no hope for them. Because of what Adam did, "sin entered into the world and death through sin, and so death spread to all men because they had all sinned." (Romans 5:12) When Adam sinned, he "sold" himself and us into slavery to sin and death. (Romans 7:14) Is there any hope for us? Yes, there is.

---

5. What does it mean when the Bible says that Adam was made "in God's image"?
6. When Adam disobeyed God, what did he lose? How does this affect us?

7 What is a ransom? The idea of a ransom basically involves two things. First, a ransom is the price paid to release someone or to buy something back. Second, a ransom is the price that covers, or pays, the cost of something.

8 No human could pay for the enormous damage that Adam did when he sinned and brought death upon us. But Jehovah provided the way to free us from sin and death. Let us learn how the ransom works and how we can benefit from it.

HOW JEHOVAH PROVIDED THE RANSOM

9 None of us could ever pay the ransom for the perfect life that Adam lost. Why not? Because all of us are imperfect. (Psalm 49:7, 8) The ransom that had to be paid was another perfect human life. That is why it is called "a corresponding ransom." (1 Timothy 2:6) The ransom had to have the same value as the life that Adam lost.

10 How did Jehovah provide the ransom? Jehovah sent his most precious Son to the earth. This Son, Jesus, was his very first creation. (1 John 4:9, 10) Jesus was willing to leave his Father and his home in heaven. (Philippians 2:7) Jehovah transferred Jesus from heaven to earth, and Jesus was born as a perfect human, without sin.—Luke 1:35.

11 The first man, Adam, lost perfect life for all hu-

7, 8. What is a ransom?
9. How could the ransom be paid?
10. How did Jehovah provide the ransom?
11. How could one man be the ransom for all humans?

mans when he disobeyed Jehovah. Could another man remove death for all of Adam's children? Yes. **(Read Romans 5:19.)** Jesus, who never sinned, gave his perfect life as the ransom. (1 Corinthians 15:45) His perfect life could be used to remove death for all of Adam's children.—1 Corinthians 15: 21, 22.

12 The Bible describes how much Jesus suffered before he died. He was cruelly whipped, nailed to a torture stake, and made to endure a slow and painful death. (John 19:1, 16-18, 30) Why did Jesus have to suffer so much? Because Satan claimed that no human would be loyal to God if he was severely tested. Jesus proved that a perfect man can be loyal to God even if he suffers to the extreme. Imagine how proud Jehovah was of Jesus!—Proverbs 27:11; see Endnote 15.

13 How was the ransom paid? Jesus gave his Father the value of his life. In the year 33, on Nisan 14 of the Jewish calendar, Jehovah allowed Jesus' enemies to kill him. (Hebrews 10:10) Three days after that, Jehovah brought Jesus back to life, not as a human, but as a spirit person. Later, when Jesus returned to his Father in heaven, he presented the value of his perfect human life to Jehovah as the ransom. (Hebrews 9:24) Now that the ransom has been paid, we have the opportunity to be set free from sin and death.—**Read Romans 3:23, 24.**

---

12. Why did Jesus have to suffer so much?
13. How was the ransom paid?

HOW YOU CAN BENEFIT FROM
THE RANSOM

14 We already benefit from God's greatest gift. Let us see how we benefit now and how we will benefit in the future.

15 **Our sins are forgiven.** It is hard to do what is right all the time. We make mistakes, and we sometimes say and do the wrong thing. (Colossians 1:13, 14) How can we be forgiven? We should be truly sorry for what we have done wrong and humbly ask Jehovah to forgive us. We can then have the confidence that our sins are forgiven.—1 John 1:8, 9.

16 **We can have a good conscience.** If our conscience tells us that we have done something wrong, we feel guilty, maybe even hopeless and worthless. But there is no need to give up. If we beg Jehovah for forgiveness, we can be sure that he will listen to us and forgive us. (Hebrews 9:13, 14) Jehovah wants us to talk to him about any of our problems and weaknesses. (Hebrews 4:14-16) As a result, we can be at peace with God.

17 **We have the hope of living forever.** "The wages sin pays is death, but the gift God gives is everlasting life by Christ Jesus our Lord." (Romans 6:23) Because Jesus died for us, we can live forever and enjoy perfect health. (Revelation 21:3, 4) But what must we do to receive those blessings?

14, 15. What must we do for our sins to be forgiven?
16. What must we do to have a good conscience?
17. What blessings are possible because Jesus died for us?

ΙΗϹΟΥϹΟΝΑΖΩΡΑΙΟϹ
ΟΒΑϹΙΛΕΥϹ ΤΩΝΙΟΥΔΑΙΩΝ

Jehovah gave
his precious Son
as a ransom for us

WILL YOU ACCEPT THE RANSOM?

18 Think of how your heart is touched when someone gives you a beautiful gift. The ransom is the most precious gift of all, and we should be deeply grateful to Jehovah for it. John 3:16 tells us that "God loved the world so much that he gave his only-begotten Son." Yes, Jehovah loves us so much that he gave us his precious Son, Jesus. And we know that Jesus also loves us, because he was willing to die for us. (John 15:13) The gift of the ransom should convince you that Jehovah and Jesus really love you.—Galatians 2:20.

19 Now that you've learned about God's great love, how can you become his friend? It is not easy to love someone you don't know. John 17:3 says that we can **come to know Jehovah.** As you do this, your love for him will deepen, you will want to please him, and you will become his friend. So keep learning about Jehovah by studying the Bible.—1 John 5:3.

20 **Accept Jesus' ransom sacrifice.** The Bible says that "the one who exercises faith in the Son has everlasting life." (John 3:36) What does it mean to exercise faith? It means to do what Jesus taught us to do. (John 13:15) We cannot simply say that we believe in Jesus. To accept the ransom, we must do something about our faith. At James 2:26, we read: "Faith without works is dead."

18. How do we know that Jehovah loves us?
19, 20. (a) How can you become Jehovah's friend? (b) How can you show that you accept Jesus' ransom sacrifice?

As we learn about Jehovah, we will become his friend and our love for him will deepen

21 Attend the Memorial of Christ's death. The evening before Jesus died, he taught us that we should have a memorial of his death. We do this each year, and it is called the Memorial or "the Lord's Evening Meal." (1 Corinthians 11:20; Matthew 26:26-28) Jesus wants us to remember that he gave his perfect life as a ransom for us. He said: "Keep doing this in remembrance of me." **(Read Luke 22:19.)** When you attend the Memorial, you show that you remember the ransom and the great love that Jehovah and Jesus have for us.—See Endnote 16.

22 The ransom is the greatest gift we could ever receive. (2 Corinthians 9:14, 15) That precious gift will even benefit millions of people who have already died. Chapters 6 and 7 will discuss how that is possible.

21, 22. (a) Why should we attend the Memorial of Christ's death each year? (b) What will be discussed in Chapters 6 and 7?

WE ALL NEED THE RANSOM

"The Son of man came . . . to give his life as a ransom in exchange for many."—Matthew 20:28

Why do we need the ransom?

Genesis 3:17-19
When Adam disobeyed God, he lost his special friendship with Jehovah, his perfect life, and his Paradise home.

Romans 5:12
Because of what Adam did, we inherited sin and death.

Ephesians 1:7
The ransom is Jehovah's way of freeing humans from sin and death.

JEHOVAH PROVIDED THE RANSOM

"God sent his only-begotten Son into the world so that we might gain life through him."—1 John 4:9

How did Jehovah provide the ransom?

Psalm 49:7, 8
None of us could ever pay the ransom for the perfect life that Adam lost.

Luke 1:35
Jehovah sent his precious Son to the earth to be born as a perfect human.

**Romans 3:23, 24;
Hebrews 9:24**
After Jesus was resurrected, he returned to heaven, where he gave the value of his perfect human life to Jehovah as the ransom.

TRUTH 3

THE RANSOM GIVES US REAL HOPE

"He will wipe out every tear from their eyes, and death will be no more."—Revelation 21:4

How can we benefit from the ransom?

1 John 1:8, 9
Our sins can be forgiven.

Hebrews 9:13, 14
We can have a clean conscience before God.

Romans 6:23
We have the hope of everlasting life.

Galatians 2:20
The gift of the ransom proves that Jehovah and Jesus really love us.

TRUTH 4

WE NEED TO ACCEPT THE RANSOM

"God . . . gave his only-begotten Son, so that everyone exercising faith in him might . . . have everlasting life."—John 3:16

How can we show we are grateful for God's gift of the ransom?

John 17:3
Come to know Jehovah and Jesus, and imitate them.

Luke 22:19
Attend the Memorial of Christ's death each year.

John 3:36; James 2:26
Do more than simply say we believe in Jesus. Do what Jesus taught us to do.

CHAPTER SIX

WHERE DO WE GO WHEN WE DIE?

THE Bible promises us that one day "death will be no more." (Revelation 21:4) In Chapter 5, we learned that the ransom makes it possible for us to have everlasting life. But people still die. (Ecclesiastes 9:5) So one of the big questions we ask is, What happens to us when we die?

² The answer to that question is especially important when someone we love dies. We may wonder: 'Where has he gone? Is he watching us? Can he help us? Will we ever see him again?'

³ Religions answer those questions in different ways. Some teach that if you are a good person, you go to heaven and that if you are a bad person, you burn in hell. Some say that when you die you become a spirit and live with your family members who have already died. And others say that after you have died and are judged, you will be reborn, or come back to life with a different body, perhaps as another person or even an animal.

⁴ Religions seem to teach very different things. But almost all of them teach one basic idea. They teach that when a human dies, a part of him keeps on living. Is that true?

1-3. What questions do people ask about death, and how do some religions answer them?
4. What basic idea do religions teach about death?

WHERE DO WE GO WHEN WE DIE?

5 Jehovah knows what happens to us when we die, and he has told us that **when a person dies, his life ends.** Death is the opposite of life. So when someone dies, his feelings and memories **do not** keep on living somewhere else.* When we die we can't see, we can't hear, and we can't think anymore.

6 King Solomon wrote that "the dead know **nothing at all.**" The dead cannot love or hate, and "there is no work nor planning nor knowledge nor wisdom in the Grave." **(Read Ecclesiastes 9:5, 6, 10.)** And at Psalm 146:4, the Bible tells us that when someone dies, "his thoughts" die.

WHAT JESUS SAID ABOUT DEATH

7 When his good friend Lazarus died, Jesus said to his disciples: "Lazarus our friend has fallen asleep." But Jesus didn't mean that Lazarus was resting. Jesus further said: "Lazarus has died." (John 11:11-14) So Jesus compared death to sleep. He didn't say that Lazarus was in heaven or with his family members who had died. And he didn't say that Lazarus was suffering in hell or being reborn as another human or an animal. No, it was as if Lazarus were in a deep sleep. Other scriptures compare death to a deep sleep. The Bible says that when Stephen was killed, "he fell asleep in death." (Acts 7:60) The apostle Paul

---

* Some people believe that a soul or spirit keeps living after someone dies. For more information, see Endnotes 17 and 18.

5, 6. What happens to us when we die?
7. What did Jesus say about death?

also wrote that some Christians had "fallen asleep in death."—1 Corinthians 15:6.

8 Did God create Adam and Eve so that they would eventually die? No! Jehovah created them to enjoy life forever with perfect health. When Jehovah made humans, he gave them the desire to live forever. (Ecclesiastes 3:11) Parents do not want to see their children grow old and die, and Jehovah feels the same way about us. But if God created us to live forever, why do we die?

8. How do we know that God did not create humans to die?

Jehovah created humans to live forever on earth

WHY DO WE DIE?

9 In the garden of Eden, Jehovah told Adam: "From every tree of the garden you may eat to satisfaction. But as for the tree of the knowledge of good and bad, you must not eat from it, for in the day you eat from it you will certainly die." (Genesis 2:9, 16, 17) That clear command was not difficult to obey, and Jehovah had the right to tell Adam and Eve what is good and what is bad. By obeying Jehovah, they would show him that they respected his authority. They would also show him just how thankful they were for everything he had given them.

10 Sadly, Adam and Eve chose to disobey Jehovah. Satan said to Eve: "Did God really say that you must not eat from every tree of the garden?" Eve replied: "We may eat of the fruit of the trees of the garden. But God has said about the fruit of the tree that is in the middle of the garden: 'You must not eat from it, no, you must not touch it; otherwise you will die.'" —Genesis 3:1-3.

11 Then Satan said: "You certainly will not die. For God knows that in the very day you eat from it, your eyes will be opened and you will be like God, knowing good and bad." (Genesis 3:4-6) Satan wanted Eve to think that she could decide for herself what was good and what was bad. At the same time, he lied

---

9. Why was the command that Jehovah gave to Adam and Eve reasonable?

10, 11. (a) How did Satan mislead Adam and Eve? (b) Why is there no excuse for what Adam and Eve did?

about what would happen if she disobeyed. Satan said that Eve wouldn't die, so Eve ate some of the fruit and then gave some to her husband. Adam and Eve knew that Jehovah had told them **not** to eat the fruit. When they ate it, they chose to disobey a clear and reasonable command. By eating, they showed that they did not respect their loving heavenly Father. There is no excuse for what they did!

¹² How disappointing that our first parents had such disrespect for their Creator! How would you feel if you worked hard to raise a son and a daughter and then they rebelled against you and did the opposite of what you asked them to do? Wouldn't it break your heart?

¹³ When they disobeyed, Adam and Eve lost the opportunity to live forever. Jehovah had told Adam: "For dust you are and to dust you will return." **(Read Genesis 3:19.)** That meant that Adam would become dust again, as if he had never been created. (Genesis 2:7) After Adam sinned, he died and no longer existed.

Adam came from the dust, and he returned to the dust

---

12. Why is it so disappointing that Adam and Eve disobeyed Jehovah?
13. What did Jehovah mean when he said "to dust you will return"?

14 If Adam and Eve had obeyed God, they would still be alive today. But when they disobeyed him, they sinned, and eventually they died. Sin is like a terrible disease that we have inherited from our first parents. All of us are born as sinners, and that is why we die. (Romans 5:12) But that is not God's purpose for humans. God never wanted humans to die, and the Bible calls death an "enemy."—1 Corinthians 15:26.

THE TRUTH SETS US FREE

15 The truth about death sets us free from many wrong ideas. The Bible teaches us that the dead don't feel pain or sadness. We can't speak to them, and they can't speak to us. We can't help the dead, and the dead can't help us. They can't harm us, so we don't need to be afraid of them. However, many religions tell us that the dead are alive somewhere and that we can help them if we pay money to priests or those viewed as holy men. But when we know the truth about death, we are not fooled by those lies.

16 Satan uses false religion to lie to us and make us think that the dead are still alive. For example, some religions teach that when we die, a part of us keeps on living somewhere else. Does your religion teach you that, or does it teach you what the Bible says about the dead? Satan uses lies to turn people away from Jehovah.

14. Why do we die?
15. How does the truth about death set us free?
16. What lie do many religions teach about the dead?

17 What many religions teach is shocking. For example, some teach that bad people will burn forever in hell. That lie is an insult to Jehovah. He would never allow people to suffer that way! **(Read 1 John 4:8.)** How would you feel about someone who punishes a child by burning the child's hands in a fire? You would think he is very cruel. You would not want to get to know him. And that is exactly how Satan wants us to feel about Jehovah!

18 Some religions tell us that when people die, they become spirits. Such religions teach that we must respect and even be afraid of those spirits because they can become either powerful friends or terrible enemies. Many people believe that lie. They fear the dead, so they worship them instead of Jehovah. Remember that the dead cannot feel or sense anything, so we don't have to be afraid of them. Jehovah is our Creator. He is the true God, and we should worship only him.—Revelation 4:11.

19 When we know the truth about death, we are set free from religious lies. And this truth helps us to understand the wonderful promises that Jehovah has made about our life and our future.

20 A long time ago, a servant of God named Job asked: "If a man dies, can he live again?" (Job 14:14) Is it really possible for a person who is dead to live again? The answer God gives us in the Bible is very exciting. We will see it in the next chapter.

---

17. Why does the idea of people burning in hell insult Jehovah?
18. Why shouldn't we fear the dead?
19. How does knowing the truth about death help us?
20. What will we learn in the next chapter?

TRUTH 1   WHEN A PERSON DIES, HIS LIFE ENDS

"The dead know nothing at all."—Ecclesiastes 9:5

What happens to us when we die?

Psalm 146:3, 4;
Ecclesiastes 9:6, 10
When we die we cannot see, we cannot hear, and we cannot think.

John 11:11-14
Jesus compared death to sleep.

TRUTH 2   JEHOVAH NEVER WANTED HUMANS TO DIE

"As for the tree of the knowledge of good and bad, you must not eat from it, for in the day you eat from it you will certainly die."—Genesis 2:17

Why do we die?

Genesis 3:1-6
Satan lied about what would happen to Eve if she disobeyed God's command. When Adam and Eve disobeyed Jehovah, they sinned and eventually died.

Genesis 3:19
After Adam died, he no longer existed.

Romans 5:12
Sin is like a terrible disease that we have inherited from our first parents. We are all born as sinners, and that is why we die.

1 Corinthians 15:26
The Bible calls death an enemy.

TRUTH 3   # THE TRUTH ABOUT DEATH SETS US FREE

"If a man dies, can he live again? I will wait . . . until my relief comes."—Job 14:14

How does knowing the truth about death set us free from wrong ideas?

1 John 4:8
The teaching of hellfire is an insult to Jehovah. He would never allow people to suffer that way.

Revelation 4:11
Many people fear the dead, so they fear and worship them instead of Jehovah. Jehovah is the true God, and we should worship only him.

CHAPTER SEVEN

THERE WILL BE A RESURRECTION!

IMAGINE that you have been sentenced to life in prison for a crime you didn't commit. There is no chance of your ever being released. Your future seems hopeless, and there is nothing you can do about it. But just when you've lost all hope, you find out that someone has the power to release you and that he has promised to help you! How would you feel?

2 We are all prisoners of death. No matter what we do, there is no escape. But Jehovah has the power to release us from death. And he has promised that "the last enemy, death, is to be brought to nothing." —1 Corinthians 15:26.

3 Imagine the relief you will feel when you don't have to worry about dying! But Jehovah will not only remove death. He will also bring those who have already died back to life. Think what that will mean for you. He promises that those "powerless in death" will live again. (Isaiah 26:19) This is what the Bible calls the resurrection.

WHEN A LOVED ONE DIES

4 When a family member or a close friend dies, our

1-3. What has imprisoned all of us, and how will Jehovah release us?
4. (a) What can give us comfort when a family member or a friend dies? (b) Who were some of Jesus' close friends?

pain and grief can be unbearable. We feel helpless. There's nothing we can do to bring that person back to life. But the Bible gives us real comfort. **(Read 2 Corinthians 1:3, 4.)** Let us consider one example that shows how much Jehovah and Jesus want to bring our loved ones back to life. When Jesus was on earth, he often visited Lazarus and his sisters, Martha and Mary. All three were good friends of Jesus. The Bible says: "Jesus loved Martha and her sister and Lazarus." Then one day Lazarus died.—John 11:3-5.

⁵ Jesus went to comfort Martha and Mary. When Martha heard that Jesus was coming, she went outside the city to meet him. She was happy to see Jesus, but she said to him: "If you had been here, my brother would not have died." Martha thought that Jesus was too late. After that, Jesus saw her sister, Mary, crying. Seeing their sadness, he felt hurt and cried. (John 11:21, 33, 35) He felt the deep pain that comes when we lose someone we love.

⁶ Knowing that Jesus feels the way we do about death is a comfort to us. And Jesus is just like his Father. (John 14:9) Jehovah has the power to remove death forever, and that is what he will do very soon.

"LAZARUS, COME OUT!"

⁷ When Jesus arrived at the grave where Lazarus' body had been placed, the entrance had been sealed

---

5, 6. (a) What did Jesus do when he saw Lazarus' family and friends grieving? (b) Why is it comforting to know how Jesus felt about death?

7, 8. Why did Martha not want the stone to be removed from Lazarus' tomb, but what did Jesus do?

with a large stone. Jesus said: "Take the stone away." But Martha didn't want them to. Lazarus' body had already been in the tomb for four days. (John 11:39) She did not know what Jesus was about to do to help her brother.

8 Jesus said to Lazarus: "Come out!" What Martha and Mary saw next was amazing. "The man who had been dead came out with his feet and hands bound with wrappings." (John 11:43, 44) Lazarus had been brought back to life! He was reunited with his family and friends. They could hold him, touch him, and talk to him. What a miracle! Jesus had resurrected Lazarus.

"LITTLE GIRL, I SAY TO YOU, 'GET UP!'"

9 Did Jesus resurrect people by his own power? No. Before he resurrected Lazarus, Jesus prayed to Jehovah, and Jehovah gave him the power to resurrect Lazarus. **(Read John 11:41, 42.)** Lazarus wasn't the only person who was resurrected. The Bible tells us about a 12-year-old girl who was very sick. Her father, Jairus, was desperate, and he begged Jesus to heal her. She was his only child. While he was talking to Jesus, some men came up and said: "Your daughter died! Why bother the Teacher any longer?" But Jesus said to Jairus: "Have no fear, only have faith, and she will be saved." He then walked to Jairus' home with him. As they came near the house, Jesus could see and hear people crying. Jesus told them:

9, 10. (a) Who gave Jesus the power to resurrect people? (b) Why are the resurrection accounts valuable to us?

"Stop weeping, for she did not die but is sleeping."
Her father and mother must have wondered what Jesus meant. Jesus asked everyone to leave and took
her father and mother into the room where their little girl was lying. Jesus gently took her by the hand
and said to her: "Little girl, I say to you, 'Get up!'"
Imagine the joy of her parents when she immediately got up and started walking! Jesus had resurrected
their daughter. (Mark 5:22-24, 35-42; Luke 8:49-56)
From that day on, when they saw their little girl, they
would remember what Jehovah had done for them
through Jesus.*

10 Those whom Jesus brought back to life died
again later. But what we read about these people is
valuable because it gives us real hope. Jehovah wants
to resurrect people, and he will.

WHAT WE LEARN FROM
THE RESURRECTION ACCOUNTS

11 The Bible clearly says that "the dead know nothing at all." That was true of Lazarus. (Ecclesiastes 9:5)
Just as Jesus said, it was as if Lazarus had been sleeping. (John 11:11) While he was in the grave, Lazarus
knew "nothing at all."

12 When Jesus resurrected Lazarus, many people

---

* In other accounts, the Bible tells us about the resurrections of
young and old, male and female, and Israelite and foreigner. You
can read them at 1 Kings 17:17-24; 2 Kings 4:32-37; 13:20, 21; Matthew 28:5-7; Luke 7:11-17; 8:40-56; Acts 9:36-42; 20:7-12.

---

11. What does Ecclesiastes 9:5 teach us about Lazarus?
12. How do we know that the resurrection of Lazarus really happened?

The apostle Peter resurrected the Christian woman Dorcas.
—Acts 9:36-42

Elijah resurrected a widow's son.
—1 Kings 17:17-24

Imagine the joy of Lazarus' family and friends when he was resurrected!
—John 11:38-44

saw it. Even Jesus' enemies knew that he had performed this miracle. Lazarus was alive, and this proved that the resurrection really happened. (John 11:47) Also, many people went to visit Lazarus, and as a result, they started to believe that Jesus had been sent by God. Jesus' enemies didn't like that, so they planned to kill both Jesus and Lazarus.—John 11:53; 12:9-11.

13 Jesus said that "all those in the memorial tombs" will be resurrected. (John 5:28) This means that all those whom Jehovah remembers will come back to life. But for Jehovah to resurrect someone, he has to remember everything about that person. Can he really do that? Well, there are billions of stars in the universe. The Bible says that Jehovah knows the name of every single star. **(Read Isaiah 40:26.)** If he can remember the name of each star, then surely he can easily remember everything about all those he will bring back to life. More important, Jehovah created everything, so we know that he has the power to bring people back to life.

14 The faithful man Job believed in the resurrection. He asked: "If a man dies, can he live again?" Then he said to Jehovah: "You will call, and I will answer you. You will long for the work of your hands." Yes, Job knew that Jehovah is looking forward to the time when he will resurrect the dead. —Job 14:13-15.

---

13. Why can we be sure that Jehovah will resurrect the dead?
14, 15. What do Job's words teach us about the resurrection?

15 How does the hope of the resurrection make you feel? You may be wondering, 'What about my family and friends who have died, will they be resurrected too?' It comforts us to know that Jehovah really wants to bring the dead back to life. Let us see what the Bible says about where they will live and who will be resurrected.

THEY "WILL HEAR HIS VOICE AND COME OUT"

16 In the past, those who were resurrected were reunited with their family and friends here on earth. This will also happen in the future, but it will be much better. Why? Because those who are brought back to life on earth will have the opportunity to live forever and never die again. And they will live in a world very different from the one we live in today. There will be no war, no crime, and no sickness.

17 Who will be resurrected? Jesus said that "all those in the memorial tombs will hear his voice and come out." (John 5:28, 29) And Revelation 20:13 tells us: "The sea gave up the dead in it, and death and the Grave gave up the dead in them." Yes, billions of people will live again. The apostle Paul also said that both "the righteous and the unrighteous" will be resurrected. **(Read Acts 24:15.)** What does that mean?

18 "The righteous" include faithful servants of

16. What kind of life will those who are resurrected to life on earth enjoy?
17. Who will be resurrected?
18. Who are "the righteous" who will be resurrected?

Jehovah who lived before Jesus came to earth. People like Noah, Abraham, Sarah, Moses, Ruth, and Esther will be resurrected to life here on earth. You can read about some of those men and women in Hebrews chapter 11. What about Jehovah's faithful servants who die in our time? They are also "righteous," so they will be resurrected.

In Paradise, the dead will be resurrected and reunited with their loved ones

¹⁹ "The unrighteous" include billions of people who did not have the opportunity to know Jehovah. Even though they died, Jehovah hasn't forgotten them. He will resurrect them, and they will have the opportunity to learn about him and serve him.

²⁰ Does this mean that everyone who has died will be resurrected? No. Jesus said that some people would not be brought back to life. (Luke 12:5) Who will decide whether a person will be resurrected or not? Jehovah is the final Judge, but he has also given Jesus the authority "to be judge of the living and the dead." (Acts 10:42) Anyone who is judged as wicked and unwilling to change will not be resurrected.—See Endnote 19.

RESURRECTION TO HEAVEN

²¹ The Bible also tells us that some people will live in heaven. When someone is resurrected to heaven, he is not brought back to life as a human with a human body. He is resurrected to life in heaven as a spirit person.

²² Jesus was the first person to receive this type of resurrection. (John 3:13) Three days after Jesus was killed, Jehovah resurrected him. (Psalm 16:10; Acts 13:34, 35) Jesus was not resurrected with a human body. The apostle Peter explains that Jesus "was put to death in the flesh but made alive in the spirit."

---

19. Who are "the unrighteous"? What opportunity will Jehovah give them?
20. Why won't everyone be resurrected?
21, 22. (a) What does it mean to be resurrected to heaven? (b) Who was the first person to be resurrected to life in heaven?

(1 Peter 3:18) Jesus was brought back to life as a powerful spirit person! (1 Corinthians 15:3-6) But the Bible says that he would not be the only one.

23 Just before he died, Jesus told his faithful disciples: "I am going my way to prepare a place for you." (John 14:2) This means that some of his followers would be resurrected to live with him in heaven. How many? Jesus said that it would be a small number, a "little flock." (Luke 12:32) The apostle John gave the exact number when he saw Jesus "standing on [heavenly] Mount Zion, and with him 144,000." —Revelation 14:1.

24 When would the 144,000 Christians be resurrected? The Bible tells us that this would happen after Christ started to rule in heaven. (1 Corinthians 15:23) We are living in that time right now, and most of the 144,000 have already been resurrected to heaven. Those who are still on earth and who die in our day will instantly be resurrected to life in heaven. However, the majority of people will be resurrected in the future to life in Paradise here on earth.

25 Very soon, Jehovah will free all humans from death, and death will be gone forever! **(Read Isaiah 25:8.)** But what will those who go to heaven do there? The Bible explains that they will rule with Jesus in a Kingdom government. We will learn more about that government in the next chapter.

23, 24. Who are the "little flock" that Jesus spoke about, and how many will there be?
25. What will we learn about in the next chapter?

TRUTH 1 JEHOVAH WILL REMOVE DEATH

"The last enemy, death, is to be brought to nothing."—1 Corinthians 15:26

How does the Bible give us real comfort when someone dies?

2 Corinthians 1:3, 4
When a family member or a close friend dies, we may feel helpless. The Bible gives us real comfort.

Isaiah 25:8; 26:19
Jehovah has the power to remove death forever. He will even bring those who have already died back to life.

TRUTH 2 WE CAN HAVE FAITH IN THE RESURRECTION

"Little girl, I say to you, 'Get up!' "—Mark 5:41

Why can we have faith in the resurrection?

John 11:1-44
Jesus resurrected Lazarus.

Mark 5:22-24, 35-42
Jesus resurrected a little girl.

John 11:41, 42
Jesus resurrected the dead using power from Jehovah.

John 12:9-11
Many witnesses saw Jesus resurrect the dead. Even Jesus' enemies knew that he could do that.

TRUTH 3 # JEHOVAH WILL BRING BILLIONS OF PEOPLE BACK TO LIFE

"You will call, and I will answer you. You will long for the work of your hands."—Job 14:13-15

Who will be resurrected?

John 5:28, 29
All those in Jehovah's memory will come back to life.

Acts 24:15
Righteous and unrighteous people will be resurrected.

Isaiah 40:26
Jehovah can remember the name of each star, so he can easily remember everything about those he will bring back to life.

TRUTH 4 # SOME PEOPLE ARE RESURRECTED TO LIVE IN HEAVEN

"I am going my way to prepare a place for you."
—John 14:2

Who are resurrected to life in heaven?

1 Peter 3:18
Jesus was the first person to be resurrected to life in heaven.

Luke 12:32
Jesus said that only a small number of his disciples would be resurrected to live in heaven.

Revelation 14:1
Jehovah has chosen a total of 144,000 to live in heaven.

CHAPTER EIGHT

WHAT IS GOD'S KINGDOM?

MILLIONS of people know the famous prayer called the Our Father, or the Lord's Prayer. Jesus used this prayer to teach his disciples how to pray. What did he pray for? And why is this prayer important for us today?

² Jesus said: "You must pray, then, this way: 'Our Father in the heavens, let your name be sanctified [or, be made holy]. Let your Kingdom come. Let your will take place, as in heaven, also on earth.'" **(Read Matthew 6:9-13.)** Why did Jesus teach us to pray for those three things?—See Endnote 20.

³ We have learned that God's name is Jehovah. And we have discussed what God's will is for humans and for the earth. But what did Jesus mean when he said: "Let your Kingdom come"? We will learn what God's Kingdom is, what it will do, and how it will make God's name holy.

WHAT IS GOD'S KINGDOM?

⁴ Jehovah set up a heavenly government and chose Jesus to be its King. The Bible calls this government God's Kingdom. Jesus is "the King of those who rule as kings and Lord of those who rule as

---

1. What famous prayer will we now discuss?
2. What are three important things that Jesus taught us to pray for?
3. What do we need to know about God's Kingdom?
4. What is God's Kingdom, and who is its King?

lords." (1 Timothy 6:15) Jesus is able to do more good than **any** human ruler ever could, and he is more powerful than all human rulers put together.

⁵ Forty days after his resurrection, Jesus returned to heaven. Eventually, Jehovah appointed him as King of the Kingdom. (Acts 2:33) God's government will rule over the earth from heaven. (Revelation 11:15) That's why the Bible calls God's Kingdom a "heavenly Kingdom."—2 Timothy 4:18.

⁶ The Bible says that Jesus is greater than any human king because he is "the one alone having immortality." (1 Timothy 6:16) All human rulers eventually die, but Jesus will never die. All the good that Jesus will do for us will last forever.

⁷ Bible prophecy says that Jesus will be a fair and compassionate King: "The spirit of Jehovah will settle upon him, the spirit of wisdom and of understanding, the spirit of counsel and of mightiness, the spirit of knowledge and of the fear of Jehovah. And he will find delight in the fear of Jehovah. He will not judge by what appears to his eyes, nor reprove [or, counsel] simply according to what his ears hear. He will judge the lowly [or, poor] with fairness." (Isaiah 11:2-4) Would you want your king to be like that?

⁸ God has selected some humans to rule with Jesus in the heavenly government. For example, the apos-

---

5. Where does God's government rule from? What will it rule over?
6, 7. What makes Jesus better than any human king?
8. How do we know that Jesus will not rule alone?

tle Paul told Timothy: "If we go on enduring, we will also rule together as kings." (2 Timothy 2:12) How many will rule as kings with Jesus?

⁹ As we learned in Chapter 7, the apostle John was given a vision where he saw Jesus as King in heaven with 144,000 other kings. Who are the 144,-000? John explains that they "have [Jesus'] name and the name of his Father written on their foreheads." And he adds: "These are the ones who keep following the Lamb [that is, Jesus] no matter where he goes. These were bought from among mankind." **(Read Revelation 14:1, 4.)** The 144,000 are faithful Christians whom God has chosen "to rule as kings over the earth" with Jesus. When they die, they are resurrected to life in heaven. (Revelation 5:10) Since the time of the apostles, Jehovah has been choosing faithful Christians to be part of that group of 144,000 kings.

¹⁰ Jehovah cares for us so much that he has arranged for humans to rule with Jesus. Jesus will be a good ruler because he understands us. He knows what it's like to be a human and to suffer. Paul said that Jesus feels for us, he can "sympathize with our weaknesses," and he "has been tested in all respects as we have." (Hebrews 4:15; 5:8) The 144,000 also know what it's like to be human. And they have struggled with imperfection and sickness. So we can

---

9. How many will rule with Jesus? When did God start to choose them?
10. Why is it loving of Jehovah to have Jesus and the 144,000 rule over humans?

be sure that Jesus and the 144,000 will understand not only how we feel but also the problems we have to deal with.

WHAT WILL GOD'S KINGDOM DO?

¹¹ Jesus taught his disciples to pray for God's will to take place in heaven. Why? We learned in Chapter 3 that Satan the Devil rebelled against Jehovah. After Satan rebelled, Jehovah allowed him and the unfaithful angels, or demons, to stay in heaven for a time. So not all in heaven were doing God's will. In Chapter 10, we will learn more about Satan and the demons.

¹² The Bible explains that soon after Jesus was made King of God's Kingdom, he would go to war against Satan. (Read Revelation 12:7-10.) Verse 10 describes two very important events. God's Kingdom begins to rule with Jesus Christ as King, and Satan is thrown out of heaven down to the earth. As we will learn, these events have already happened.

¹³ The Bible describes the joy of the faithful angels after Satan and his demons were thrown out of heaven. We read: "Be glad, you heavens and you who reside in them!" (Revelation 12:12) There is now total peace and unity in heaven because everyone there is doing God's will.

----

11. Why did Jesus teach his disciples to pray for God's will to take place in heaven?
12. What two important events are described at Revelation 12:10?
13. What happened in heaven when Satan was thrown out?

14 But life on earth is very different. Terrible things happen to people "because the Devil has come down" and he has "great anger, knowing that he has a short period of time." (Revelation 12:12) Satan is furious. He has been thrown out of heaven, and he knows he will be destroyed very soon. He does everything he can to cause trouble, pain, and suffering all over the earth.

15 But God's will for the earth has not changed. He still wants perfect humans to live forever on a paradise earth. (Psalm 37:29) So how will God's Kingdom make this possible?

16 The prophecy at Daniel 2:44 says: "In the days of those kings the God of heaven will set up a kingdom that will never be destroyed. And this kingdom will not be passed on to any other people. It will crush and put an end to all these kingdoms, and it alone will stand forever." What does this prophecy teach us about God's Kingdom?

17 First, it tells us that God's Kingdom would begin ruling "in the days of those kings." This means that other governments would still exist on the earth when the Kingdom started to rule. Second, it tells us that God's Kingdom would last forever and never be replaced by another government. And third, there would be war between God's Kingdom and the governments of this world. God's Kingdom would win

---

14. What has happened on the earth because Satan was thrown out of heaven?
15. What is God's will for the earth?
16, 17. What does Daniel 2:44 tell us about God's Kingdom?

and become the only government ruling over the earth. Then humans will have the best government they could ever have.

18 How will God's Kingdom take over the rulership of the earth? Before the final war, called the war of Armageddon, the demons will mislead "the kings of the entire inhabited earth, to gather them together to the war of the great day of God the Almighty." Yes, human governments will fight against God's Kingdom.—Revelation 16:14, 16; see Endnote 10.

19 Why do we need God's Kingdom? There are at least three reasons. First, we are sinners, so we get sick and die. But the Bible says that under God's Kingdom, we will live forever. In fact, John 3:16 says: "God loved the world so much that he gave his only-begotten Son, so that everyone exercising faith in him might not be destroyed but have everlasting life."

20 A second reason why we need God's Kingdom is that we are surrounded by wicked people. Many lie and cheat and are immoral. We can't do anything to remove them, but God will. People who keep doing wicked things will be destroyed during Armageddon. **(Read Psalm 37:10.)** A third reason why we need God's Kingdom is that human governments have been weak, cruel, or corrupt. They are not interested in helping people to obey God. The Bible says

---

18. What is the name of the final war between God's Kingdom and the governments of this world?
19, 20. Why do we need God's Kingdom to rule over the earth?

Since Satan and his demons were thrown out of heaven, there has been more suffering on earth. This suffering will soon end

that "man has dominated man to his harm."—Ecclesiastes 8:9.

21 After Armageddon, God's Kingdom will make sure that God's will is done on earth. For example, it will remove Satan and his demons. (Revelation 20:1-3) Eventually, nobody will get sick or die. Because of the ransom, all faithful humans will be able to live forever in Paradise. (Revelation 22:1-3) The Kingdom will sanctify God's name. What does this mean? It means that when God's government rules the earth, all humans will honor Jehovah's name.—See Endnote 21.

WHEN DID JESUS BECOME KING?

22 Jesus taught his disciples to pray: "Let your Kingdom come." So it was obvious that God's government would come in the future. Jehovah would first establish his government and make Jesus its

---

21. How will the Kingdom make sure that God's will is done on earth?
22. How do we know that Jesus did not become King when he was on earth or immediately after he was resurrected?

God's Kingdom will make sure that
God's will is done on earth

King. Was Jesus made King as soon as he returned to heaven? No, he would have to wait. Some time after Jesus' resurrection, both Peter and Paul made this clear when they applied the prophecy at Psalm 110:1 to Jesus. In the prophecy Jehovah says: "Sit at my right hand until I place your enemies as a stool for your feet." (Acts 2:32-35; Hebrews 10:12, 13) How long would Jesus need to wait before Jehovah would make him King?

²³ For many years before 1914, a group of sincere Christians understood that it would be an important year in Bible prophecy. World events since 1914 have proved that they were correct. Jesus began to rule as King in that year. (Psalm 110:2) Soon after that, Satan was thrown down to the earth, and now "he has a short period of time." (Revelation 12:12) In the next chapter, we will see more evidence that we are living in that time period. We will also learn that very soon God's Kingdom will make sure that God's will is done on earth.—See Endnote 22.

23. (a) When did Jesus begin to rule as King of God's government? (b) What will we learn in the next chapter?

TRUTH 1 ## GOD'S KINGDOM IS A REAL GOVERNMENT

"Let your Kingdom come. Let your will take place, as in heaven, also on earth."—Matthew 6:9-13

What is God's Kingdom?

Revelation 11:15
God's Kingdom, or government, will rule over the earth from heaven.

1 Timothy 6:15
Jesus is the King of God's Kingdom.

Revelation 14:1, 4
144,000 humans will rule with Jesus from heaven.

Hebrews 4:15; 5:8
Jesus and the 144,000 understand how we feel and the problems we deal with.

TRUTH 2 ## JESUS WILL BE THE BEST RULER

"He will judge the lowly [or, poor] with fairness."
—Isaiah 11:4

Why is Jesus the best choice to be King of the Kingdom?

1 Timothy 6:16
All human rulers eventually die, but Jesus will never die. All the good that Jesus will do for us will last forever.

Isaiah 11:2-4
Jesus is able to do more good than any human ruler could. He is more powerful than all human rulers put together. He is fair and compassionate.

TRUTH 3

GOD'S KINGDOM WILL MAKE SURE THAT GOD'S WILL IS DONE

"The God of heaven will set up a kingdom that will never be destroyed."—Daniel 2:44

What has the Kingdom already done? What will it do in the future?

Revelation 12:7-12
After Jesus was made King in 1914, he threw Satan out of heaven and down to the earth. That is why there is so much trouble, pain, and suffering all over the earth.

Ecclesiastes 8:9; Revelation 16:16
At Armageddon, God's Kingdom will destroy all the cruel and corrupt human governments.

Psalm 37:10
People who keep doing wicked things will be destroyed.

Revelation 22:1-3
When God's Kingdom rules the earth, nobody will get sick or die and all humans will honor God's name.

CHAPTER NINE

IS THE END OF THE WORLD NEAR?

HAVE you ever watched the news and thought, 'Can things get any worse?' There is so much tragedy and cruelty that some people believe we must be close to the end of the world. Is that true? Is there a way to know what will happen in the future? Yes. Although humans cannot predict what will happen, Jehovah God can. He tells us in the Bible about our future and the earth's future.—Isaiah 46:10; James 4:14.

2 When we read in the Bible about the end of the world, it means, not the end of planet Earth, but the end of wickedness. Jesus taught people that the Kingdom of God would rule over the earth. (Luke 4:43) His disciples wanted to know when God's Kingdom would come, and they asked Jesus: "When will these things be, and what will be the sign of your presence and of the conclusion of the system of things?" (Matthew 24:3) Jesus did not give them the exact date, but he told them what would happen just before the end of this world. What Jesus said would happen is happening right now.

3 In this chapter we will discuss evidence that we are living in the time just before the end of the world. First, we need to learn about a war that took

---

1. Where can we learn about the future?
2, 3. What did Jesus' disciples want to know, and how did Jesus answer them?

place in heaven so that we can understand why things are so bad here on earth.

A WAR IN HEAVEN

4 In Chapter 8 we learned that Jesus became King in heaven in 1914. (Daniel 7:13, 14) The book of Revelation tells us what happened: "War broke out in heaven: Michael [meaning, Jesus] and his angels battled with the dragon [Satan], and the dragon and its angels battled."* Satan and his demons lost the war and were thrown down to the earth. Imagine the joy that the angels felt! But what about the people on earth? The Bible says that it would be a time of trouble for mankind. Why? Because the Devil is very angry, "knowing that he has a short period of time." —Revelation 12:7, 9, 12.

5 The Devil is causing as much trouble as he can on earth. He's furious because he has a short time left before God removes him. Let us examine what Jesus said would happen during the last days.—See Endnote 24.

THE LAST DAYS

6 **War.** Jesus said: "Nation will rise against nation and kingdom against kingdom." (Matthew 24:7)

---

* Michael is another name for Jesus Christ. For more information, please see Endnote 23.

4, 5. (a) What happened in heaven soon after Jesus became King? (b) According to Revelation 12:12, what would happen on earth after Satan was thrown down?

6, 7. What can be said about war and hunger today?

More people have been killed in wars in our time than at any other time in history. One report from the Worldwatch Institute shows that since 1914, wars have killed more than 100 million people. More than three times as many people were killed in wars during the 100 years between 1900 and 2000 as were killed during the previous 1,900 years. Just imagine the misery and pain that millions of people have felt because of war!

⁷ **Hunger.** Jesus said: "There will be food shortages." (Matthew 24:7) Even though more food is produced now than ever before, many people never have enough to eat. Why? Because they don't have enough money to buy food or land on which to grow it. More than a billion people have less than one dollar a day to live on. The World Health Organization says that millions of children die each year, mainly because they don't have enough food to keep them healthy.

8 Earthquakes. Jesus prophesied: "There will be great earthquakes." (Luke 21:11) Many powerful earthquakes are now expected every year. Since the year 1900, over two million people have died because of earthquakes. And although technology has helped to detect earthquakes earlier than before, many people still die.

9 Disease. Jesus foretold that there would be "pestilences." Dangerous diseases would spread quickly and kill many. (Luke 21:11) Even though doctors have learned how to treat many sicknesses, there are still sicknesses that cannot be cured. In fact, one report explains that each year, millions of people die from diseases, such as tuberculosis, malaria, and cholera. Not only that, but doctors have found 30 new diseases, and some of them have no cure.

8, 9. What shows that Jesus' prophecies about earthquakes and disease have come true?

WHAT PEOPLE WOULD BE LIKE IN THE LAST DAYS

10 At 2 Timothy 3:1-5, the Bible says: "In the last days critical times hard to deal with will be here." The apostle Paul described how many people would behave during the last days. He said people would

- be selfish
- love money
- disobey their parents
- not be loyal
- lack affection for their family
- have no self-control
- be violent and aggressive
- love pleasures more than God
- pretend to love God but refuse to obey him

11 Do many people behave like this where you live? All over the world, many do. But God will soon do something about it. He promises: "When the wicked sprout like weeds and all the wrongdoers flourish, it is that

---

10. How is 2 Timothy 3:1-5 coming true today?
11. According to Psalm 92:7, what will happen to wicked people?

they may be annihilated [or, destroyed] forever."
—Psalm 92:7.

GOOD NEWS IN THE LAST DAYS

12 The Bible foretold that during the last days, the world would be full of pain and suffering. But the Bible also says that good things will happen.

13 **Understanding the Bible.** The prophet Daniel wrote about the last days. He said: "The true knowledge will become abundant." (Daniel 12:4) God would give his people the ability to understand the Bible more clearly than ever before. Jehovah has done this especially since 1914. For example, he has taught us the importance of his name and his purpose for the earth as well as the truth about the ransom, what happens when we die, and the resurrection. We have learned that only God's Kingdom can solve all our problems. We have also learned how to be happy and how to live in a way that pleases God. But what do God's servants do with what they've learned? Another prophecy gives us the answer.—See Endnotes 21 and 25.

14 **The global preaching work.** Speaking about the last days, Jesus said: "This good news of the Kingdom will be preached in all the inhabited earth." (Matthew 24:3, 14) The good news of the Kingdom is being preached in over 230 lands and in more than 700 languages. Yes, all over the earth, Jehovah's Witnesses from "all nations and tribes" are helping

---

12, 13. What has Jehovah taught us during the last days?
14. Where is the good news of the Kingdom being preached, and who are preaching it?

people to understand what the Kingdom is and what
it will do for mankind. (Revelation 7:9) And they do
this free of charge. Although they are hated and per-
secuted by many, nothing can stop the preaching
work, just as Jesus prophesied.—Luke 21:17.

WHAT WILL YOU DO?

15 Do you believe that we are living in the last
days? Many Bible prophecies about the last days are
coming true. Soon Jehovah will decide to stop the
preaching of the good news and "the end" will come.
(Matthew 24:14) What is the end? It is Armageddon,
when God will remove all wickedness. Jehovah will
use Jesus and his powerful angels to destroy anyone
who refuses to obey Him and his Son. (2 Thessalonians 1:6-9) After that, Satan and his demons will not
mislead people. And all those who want to obey God
and accept his Kingdom will see every promise of
God come true.—Revelation 20:1-3; 21:3-5.

16 This world ruled by Satan will soon come to its
end. So it is very important that we ask ourselves,
'What do I need to do?' Jehovah wants you to learn
as much as you can from the Bible. You need to take
your study seriously. (John 17:3) Jehovah's Witnesses have meetings every week to help people understand the Bible. Try to attend those meetings regularly. **(Read Hebrews 10:24, 25.)** If you learn that you
need to make changes, don't be afraid to make them.

---

15. (a) Do you believe that we are living in the last days, and why?
(b) What will happen to those who obey Jehovah and to those who
don't?
16. Since the end is so close, what do you need to do?

"This good news of the Kingdom will be preached in all the inhabited earth." —Matthew 24:14

As you make them, your friendship with Jehovah will become stronger.—James 4:8.

17 The apostle Paul explained that the destruction of the wicked will come when most people don't expect it, "as a thief in the night." (1 Thessalonians 5:2) Jesus prophesied that many would choose to ignore the evidence that we're living in the last days. He said: "Just as the days of Noah were, so the presence of the Son of man [or, the last days] will be. For as they were in those days before the Flood, eating and drinking, men marrying and women being given in marriage, until the day that Noah entered into the ark, and they took no note until the Flood came and swept them all away, so the presence of the Son of man will be."—Matthew 24:37-39.

18 Jesus warned that we should not become distracted "with overeating and heavy drinking and anxieties of life." He said that the end will come suddenly, "as a snare." He also said that it "will come upon all those dwelling on the face of the whole earth." Then he added: "Keep awake, then, all the time making supplication [or, praying very sincerely] that you may succeed in escaping all these things that must occur and in standing before the Son of man." (Luke 21:34-36) Why is it so important to listen to Jesus' warning? Because very soon Satan's wicked world will be destroyed. Only those who are approved by Jehovah and Jesus will survive the end and live forever in the new world.—John 3:16; 2 Peter 3:13.

---

17. Why will most people be surprised when the end comes?
18. What warning did Jesus give us?

SUMMARY

TRUTH 1 — JEHOVAH REVEALS THE FUTURE TO US

"From the beginning I foretell the outcome, and from long ago the things that have not yet been done."—Isaiah 46:10

What do we know about the time of the end?

Daniel 7:13, 14
Jesus became King in heaven in 1914.

Matthew 24:3-14
Jesus foretold critical times for humans.

Revelation 12:7-9, 12
Shortly after Jesus became King, he threw Satan out of the heavens to the earth. Satan is furious because he has "a short period of time" left before God removes him.

TRUTH 2 — WE ARE LIVING IN THE TIME OF THE END

"What will be the sign . . . of the conclusion of the system of things?"—Matthew 24:3

Have you seen the fulfillment of Bible prophecies?

Matthew 24:7; Luke 21:11
More than ever before, we see wars, hunger, earthquakes, and disease.

2 Timothy 3:1-5
The apostle Paul described how people would behave during the last days.

Daniel 12:4
God is helping his people to understand the Bible more clearly than ever before.

Matthew 24:14
The good news of the Kingdom is being preached all over the earth.

TRUTH 3

TAKE ACTION NOW TO PLEASE JEHOVAH

"Jehovah's day is coming exactly as a thief in the night."—1 Thessalonians 5:2

Since the end is so close, what do you need to do?

John 17:3
Take your study of the Bible seriously.

Hebrews 10:24, 25
Learn more by attending the meetings of Jehovah's Witnesses.

James 4:8
Make needed changes in your life so that you can draw closer to God.

Luke 21:34-36
Avoid distractions, and focus your life on worshipping Jehovah.

CHAPTER TEN

THE TRUTH ABOUT THE ANGELS

JEHOVAH wants us to know about his family. The angels are part of God's family. In the Bible they are called "sons of God." (Job 38:7) What do the angels do? How have they helped people in the past? And can they help us now?—See Endnote 8.

² We need to know where the angels came from. Colossians 1:16 tells us that after Jehovah created Jesus, "all other things were created in the heavens and on the earth." That includes the angels. How many of them were created? The Bible says that there are hundreds of millions of angels.—Psalm 103:20; Revelation 5:11.

³ The Bible also teaches us that Jehovah created the angels before he created the earth. How did they feel when they saw the earth? The book of Job tells us that they were joyful. They were a close family serving Jehovah together.—Job 38:4-7.

ANGELS HELP GOD'S PEOPLE

⁴ Angels have always been interested in humans and in Jehovah's purpose for the earth and humans. (Proverbs 8:30, 31; 1 Peter 1:11, 12) It must have made them very sad when Adam and Eve rebelled. They

---

1. Why learn about the angels?
2. Where did angels come from? How many angels were created?
3. What does Job 38:4-7 tell us about the angels?
4. How do we know that angels are interested in humans?

must be even sadder now to see that most humans have disobeyed Jehovah. But when someone repents and returns to God, the angels are joyful. (Luke 15: 10) The angels are very interested in those who serve God. Jehovah uses angels to help and protect his servants on earth. (Hebrews 1:7, 14) Let us look at some examples of this.

"My God sent his angel and shut the mouth of the lions."
—Daniel 6:22

⁵ Jehovah sent two angels to help Lot and his family escape the destruction of the cities of Sodom and Gomorrah. (Genesis 19:15, 16) Hundreds of years later, the prophet Daniel was thrown into a lions' pit, but he was not harmed, because "God sent his angel and shut the mouth of the lions." (Daniel 6:22) Later, when the apostle Peter was in prison, Jehovah sent an angel to set him free. (Acts 12:6-11) Angels also helped Jesus when he was on earth. For example, after he was baptized, "angels were ministering to him." (Mark 1:13) Just before Jesus was executed, an angel "strengthened him."—Luke 22:43.

⁶ Today, angels no longer appear to humans. But God still uses angels to help his servants. The Bible says: "The angel of Jehovah camps all around those fearing Him, and he rescues them." (Psalm 34:7) Why do we need protection? Because we have powerful enemies who want to harm us. Who are they? Where do they come from? How are they trying to harm us? To answer those questions, let's see what happened shortly after Adam and Eve were created.

OUR INVISIBLE ENEMIES

⁷ We learned in Chapter 3 that an angel rebelled against God and wanted to rule over others. The Bible calls him Satan the Devil. (Revelation 12:9) Satan also wanted others to rebel against God. He was able to trick Eve, and since then he has tricked most

---

5. How have angels helped God's servants in the past?
6. (a) How do we know that angels help God's people today? (b) What questions will we now answer?
7. What have people done because of Satan's tricks?

humans. However, some, such as Abel, Enoch, and Noah, remained faithful to Jehovah.—Hebrews 11:4, 5, 7.

8 In Noah's time, some angels rebelled and left their home in heaven to live as humans on earth. Why? The Bible tells us that they wanted to have wives. **(Read Genesis 6:2.)** But it was wrong for angels to do that. (Jude 6) Like those wicked angels, most humans at that time became corrupt and violent. Jehovah then decided to destroy wicked humans by flooding the whole earth. But he saved his faithful servants. (Genesis 7:17, 23) To survive, the wicked angels returned to heaven. The Bible calls those wicked angels demons. They chose to join Satan's rebellion, and the Devil became their ruler.—Matthew 9:34.

9 Because they were rebels, Jehovah did not accept the demons back into his family. (2 Peter 2:4) Demons cannot change into humans anymore, but they are still "misleading the entire inhabited earth." (Revelation 12:9; 1 John 5:19) Let us learn how they are able to trick, or mislead, so many.—**Read 2 Corinthians 2:11.**

HOW DEMONS TRICK PEOPLE

10 The demons trick people in many ways. When people contact the demons they do it either directly or through someone else, such as a witch doctor or a

8. (a) How did some angels become demons? (b) What did the demons do to survive the Flood?
9. (a) What happened to the demons when they returned to heaven? (b) What will we learn about next?
10. How do the demons trick people?

psychic. Contact with the demons is called demon-ism or spiritism. But the Bible commands us to stay far away from anything that has to do with the de-mons. (Galatians 5:19-21) Why? Just as a hunter uses a trap to catch animals, the demons use tricks to trap and control people.—See Endnote 26.

11 One of their tricks is called divination. That is the use of supernatural powers to try to find out about the future or the unknown. Someone might try to do this by looking at the stars, searching for omens, reading tarot cards, using a crystal ball, or reading the palm of a person's hand. Many people think that these practices are harmless, but they are not. They are very dangerous. For example, the Bible shows that demons and fortune-tellers work together. At Acts 16:16-18, we read about "a demon of divina-tion" who helped a girl to do "fortune-telling." After the apostle Paul sent the demon away, the girl lost her ability to foretell the future.

12 The demons use another trick to trap people. They try to make us believe that it's possible to talk to the dead and that those who have died are actual-ly still alive somewhere and can communicate with us or hurt us. For example, someone whose friend or relative has died may go to a person, such as a spirit medium, who says he or she can talk to the dead. The medium may tell the person something interesting about the dead friend or relative and even

11. What is divination, and why should we avoid it?
12. (a) Why is it dangerous to try to communicate with the dead?
(b) Why do God's servants never get involved in demonic customs?

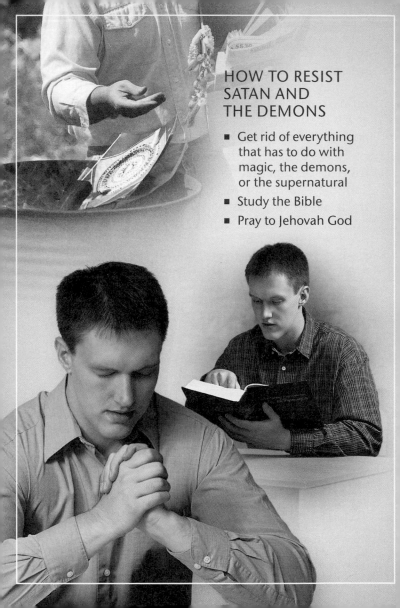

HOW TO RESIST SATAN AND THE DEMONS

- Get rid of everything that has to do with magic, the demons, or the supernatural
- Study the Bible
- Pray to Jehovah God

imitate the dead person's voice. (1 Samuel 28:3-19) Many funeral customs are also based on the belief that the dead are still alive somewhere. These may include funeral celebrations, funeral anniversaries, sacrifices for the dead, widowhood rites, or some wake rituals. When Christians refuse to take part in these customs, their families or village communities may criticize them, insult them, or refuse to have anything to do with them. But Christians know that the dead are not alive somewhere else. It's impossible to communicate with them, and they cannot harm us. (Psalm 115:17) Be very careful. Never try to communicate with the dead or the demons and never get involved in demonic customs.—**Read Deuteronomy 18:10, 11; Isaiah 8:19.**

¹³ The demons not only trick people but also frighten them. Today, Satan and his demons know that they have only "a short period of time" before God removes them from the earth, so they are more violent and aggressive than ever. (Revelation 12:12, 17) However, thousands of people who once lived in fear of the demons don't fear them anymore. How did they break free from their fear of the demons?

RESIST AND BREAK FREE FROM THE DEMONS

¹⁴ The Bible tells us how to resist the demons and how to break free from them. For example, some in the city of Ephesus were communicating with the

---

13. What have many people who once lived in fear of the demons been able to do?
14. Like Christians in the first century, how can we break free from the demons?

demons before they learned the truth. How did they break free? The Bible says: "Quite a number of those who practiced magical arts brought their books together and burned them up before everybody." (Acts 19:19) Because they wanted to be Christians, they destroyed all their books about magic. Similar action is necessary today. Everyone who wants to serve Jehovah needs to get rid of things that have anything to do with the demons. This includes books, magazines, horoscopes, movies, music, games, and even posters that make magic, demons, or the supernatural seem harmless or exciting. It also includes things that people wear to protect themselves from evil.—1 Corinthians 10:21.

15 Some years after those in Ephesus destroyed their books about magic, the apostle Paul wrote that they **still** had to "struggle" and fight "against the wicked spirit forces." (Ephesians 6:12) Yes, even though they had already burned their books, the demons were still trying to harm them. So, what else did they need to do? Paul told them: "Take up the large shield of faith, with which you will be able to extinguish [or, stop] all the wicked one's burning arrows." (Ephesians 6:16) Just as a shield protects a soldier in battle, our faith can protect us. If we have absolute confidence that Jehovah can protect us, we will be able to resist Satan and the demons.—Matthew 17:20.

16 How can we make our faith in Jehovah stronger? We need to read the Bible every day and learn to rely

---

15. What else do we need to do to resist Satan and the demons?
16. How can we make our faith in Jehovah stronger?

on him to protect us. If we have strong confidence in Jehovah, Satan and the demons will not be able to harm us.—1 John 5:5.

17 What else did the Christians in Ephesus need to do? They lived in a city full of demonism. So Paul told them: "Carry on prayer on every occasion." (Ephesians 6:18) They needed to ask Jehovah for his protection at all times. What about us? We also live in a world that is full of demonism. So we too need to ask Jehovah for his protection, and we need to use his name when we pray. **(Read Proverbs 18:10.)** If we keep on asking Jehovah to deliver us from Satan, Jehovah will answer our prayers.—Psalm 145:19; Matthew 6:13.

18 If we get rid of everything in our life that has to do with demonism and rely on Jehovah to protect us, we can resist Satan and the demons. We do not need to be afraid of them. **(Read James 4:7, 8.)** Jehovah is far more powerful than the demons. He punished them in Noah's day, and in the future he will destroy them. (Jude 6) Remember, we are not alone in our fight. Jehovah is using his angels to protect us. (2 Kings 6:15-17) We can be confident that with Jehovah's help, we can win our fight against Satan and the demons.—1 Peter 5:6, 7; 2 Peter 2:9.

19 But if Satan and the demons are causing so much suffering, why hasn't God destroyed them yet? This question will be answered in the next chapter.

---

17. What else will protect us from the demons?
18, 19. (a) How can we win our fight against Satan and the demons? (b) What question will be answered in the next chapter?

TRUTH 1 — THE ANGELS ARE PART OF GOD'S FAMILY

"Praise Jehovah, all you his angels, mighty in power."—Psalm 103:20

What do we know about the angels?

Job 38:4-7
Jehovah created the angels before he created the earth.

Revelation 5:11
There are millions of angels.

1 Peter 1:11, 12
Angels have always been interested in Jehovah's purpose for the earth.

Luke 15:10
The angels are very interested in those who serve God.

TRUTH 2 — THE ANGELS HELP GOD'S SERVANTS

"The angel of Jehovah camps all around those fearing Him, and he rescues them."—Psalm 34:7

How do we know that angels can help people?

Genesis 19:15, 16;
Daniel 6:22; Luke 22:43;
Acts 12:6-11
Angels helped Lot, Daniel, Jesus, and Peter.

Hebrews 1:7, 14
Jehovah uses his angels to help and to protect his servants today.

| TRUTH 3 | WICKED ANGELS TRY TO HARM US |

"We may not be overreached by Satan, for we are not ignorant of his designs."—2 Corinthians 2:11

Who are the demons, and why are they harmful?

Revelation 12:9
An angel rebelled against Jehovah. He is called Satan.

Genesis 6:2
In Noah's time, some angels rebelled and came to the earth.

Matthew 9:34
Those angels joined Satan's rebellion and became demons.

Deuteronomy 18:10, 11
The demons try to trick people and harm them any way they can.

| TRUTH 4 | YOU CAN RESIST SATAN AND THE DEMONS |

"Oppose the Devil, and he will flee from you."
—James 4:7

How can you have Jehovah's help in resisting Satan and the demons?

Acts 19:19
Get rid of all items connected with demonism that make magic, demons, or the supernatural seem harmless or exciting.

Ephesians 6:16, 18
Build your faith by studying the Bible, and pray for God's protection.

Proverbs 18:10
Use Jehovah's name.

CHAPTER ELEVEN

WHY SO MUCH SUFFERING?

A TSUNAMI destroys a village. A gunman opens fire in a church, wounding and killing a number of people. Cancer takes a mother's life, leaving behind five children.

² When disasters or tragedies like those happen, many people ask, "Why?" Many ask why the world is so full of hatred and suffering. Have you ever wondered about that yourself?

³ In the Bible, we learn that men who had deep faith in God also asked such questions. For example, the prophet Habakkuk asked Jehovah: "Why do you make me witness wrongdoing? And why do you tolerate oppression? Why are destruction and violence before me? And why do quarreling and conflict abound?"—Habakkuk 1:3.

⁴ At Habakkuk 2:2, 3, we read God's answer to Habakkuk's questions and His promise to correct the situation. Jehovah has deep love for people. The Bible says: "He cares for you." (1 Peter 5:7) In fact, God hates to see suffering much more than we do. (Isaiah 55:8, 9) So then, let's discuss the question, Why is there so much suffering in the world?

1, 2. What do many people ask?
3, 4. (a) What questions did Habakkuk ask? (b) How did Jehovah answer him?

WHY IS THERE SO MUCH SUFFERING?

5 Pastors, priests, and religious teachers often say that it is God's will that people suffer. Some may say that everything that happens to a person, including tragedies, has already been decided by God and that we can never understand why. Others may even say that people, including little children, die so that they can be with God in heaven. But that isn't true. Jehovah never causes bad things to happen. The Bible says: "It is unthinkable for the true God to act wickedly, for the Almighty to do wrong!"—Job 34:10.

6 Many people blame God for all the suffering in the world because they think that God rules the world. But as we learned in Chapter 3, the real ruler of the world is Satan the Devil.

7 The Bible tells us that "the whole world is lying in the power of the wicked one." (1 John 5:19) The ruler of this world, Satan, is vicious and cruel. He is "misleading the entire inhabited earth." (Revelation 12:9) Many people imitate him. And that's just one reason why the world is so full of lies, hatred, and cruelty.

8 There are other reasons why there is so much suffering in the world. After Adam and Eve rebelled, they passed sin on to their children. And because of sin, humans cause other humans to suffer. They

5. What do many religious teachers say about suffering? What does the Bible teach?
6. Why do many people blame God for all the suffering in the world?
7, 8. Why is there so much suffering in the world?

often want to be more important than others. They fight, they go to war, and they bully others. (Ecclesiastes 4:1; 8:9) Sometimes people suffer because of "time and unexpected events." (Ecclesiastes 9:11) When they are in the wrong place at the wrong time, accidents and other bad things can happen to them.

⁹ Jehovah never causes suffering. He's not to blame for war, crime, and mistreatment. God does not cause disasters such as earthquakes, hurricanes, and floods. But you may wonder, 'If Jehovah is the most powerful person in the universe, why doesn't he stop those terrible things from happening?' We know that God cares deeply about us, so he must have a very good reason for allowing suffering to continue.—1 John 4:8.

WHY GOD ALLOWS SUFFERING

¹⁰ In the garden of Eden, the Devil misled Adam and Eve. Satan accused God of being a bad Ruler. He claimed that God was keeping something good from Adam and Eve. Satan wanted them to believe that he would be a better ruler than Jehovah and that they did not need God.—Genesis 3:2-5; see Endnote 27.

¹¹ Adam and Eve disobeyed Jehovah and rebelled against him. They thought that they had the right to decide for themselves what was right and what was wrong. How could Jehovah prove that the rebels were wrong and that he knows what is best for us?

---

9. Why can we be sure that Jehovah has a very good reason for allowing suffering to continue?
10. How did Satan challenge Jehovah?
11. What question do we need to answer?

12 Jehovah didn't destroy Adam and Eve immediately. Instead, he allowed them to have children. Then Jehovah made it possible for the children of Adam and Eve to choose whom they wanted as their ruler. Jehovah's purpose was to fill the earth with perfect people, and that was going to happen no matter what the Devil tried to do.—Genesis 1:28; Isaiah 55:10, 11.

13 Satan challenged Jehovah in front of millions of angels. (Job 38:7; Daniel 7:10) So Jehovah gave Satan time to prove whether his accusation was true. He also gave humans time to set up their own governments under Satan's guidance to show whether they could be successful without God's help.

14 For thousands of years, humans have tried to rule themselves, but they have failed. Satan has been proved a liar. Humans **do need** God's help. The prophet Jeremiah was right when he said: "I well know, O Jehovah, that man's way does not belong to him. It does not belong to man who is walking even to direct his step."—Jeremiah 10:23.

WHY HAS JEHOVAH WAITED SO LONG?

15 Why has Jehovah allowed suffering to continue for so long? Why does he not stop bad things from happening? It has taken time to prove that

---

12, 13. (a) Why did Jehovah not destroy the rebels immediately? (b) Why has Jehovah allowed Satan to be the ruler of this world and humans to govern themselves?
14. What has time proved?
15, 16. (a) Why has Jehovah allowed suffering to go on for so long? (b) Why has Jehovah not fixed the problems caused by Satan?

Satan's rule has failed. Humans have tried every kind of government, without success. Even though they have made advances in science and technology, there is more injustice, poverty, crime, and war than ever before. We cannot successfully rule ourselves without God.

16 However, Jehovah has not fixed the problems caused by Satan. If he did, it would mean God supports Satan's rulership, and He will never do that. Also, humans would believe that they are able to rule themselves successfully. But that is a lie, and Jehovah would not support that either. He never lies.—Hebrews 6:18.

17 Can Jehovah repair all the damage that has been caused by the rebellion of Satan and humans? Yes. With God, all things are possible. Jehovah knows when all of Satan's challenges will have been fully answered. Then he will make the earth into a paradise, as it was meant to be. All those in "the memorial tombs" will be resurrected. (John 5:28, 29) People will never get sick or die. Jesus will undo all the damage that Satan has caused. Jehovah will use Jesus "to break up the works of the Devil." (1 John 3:8) We are grateful that in the meantime Jehovah has been patient with us so that we can come to know him and can decide that we want him to be our Ruler. **(Read 2 Peter 3:9, 10.)** Even when we suffer, he helps us to endure.—John 4:23; **read 1 Corinthians 10:13.**

_____

17, 18. What will Jehovah do about all the damage that Satan has caused?

18 Jehovah does not force us to choose him as our Ruler. He gave humans the gift of free will. Let us examine what this precious gift means to us.

HOW WILL YOU USE THE GIFT OF FREE WILL?

19 Jehovah's wonderful gift of free will makes us very different from the animals. They mainly act because of their instincts, but we can choose how we want to live our lives and decide whether we want to please Jehovah. (Proverbs 30:24) Also, we are not like machines that do only what they are made to do. We have the freedom to make choices about whom we want to be, whom we want as our friends, and what we want to do with our life. Jehovah wants us to enjoy life.

20 Jehovah wants us to love him. (Matthew 22:37, 38) He is like a father who is happy to hear his child say "I love you" when the child says it from his heart and not because he's forced to. Jehovah gave us the freedom to choose whether to serve him or not. Satan, Adam, and Eve chose to reject Jehovah. How will **you** use your gift of free will?

21 Use your free will to serve Jehovah. There are millions of others who have decided to please God and to reject Satan. (Proverbs 27:11) What can you do now so that you will be there in God's new world when he removes all suffering? The next chapter will answer that question.

---

19. What wonderful gift has Jehovah given us? Why should we be grateful for this gift?
20, 21. What is the best choice that you can make now?

TRUTH 1 — JEHOVAH DOES NOT CAUSE ANY SUFFERING

"It is unthinkable for the true God to act wickedly, for the Almighty to do wrong!"—Job 34:10

Why is there so much suffering in the world?

1 John 5:19
The ruler of the world is Satan the Devil.

Ecclesiastes 8:9
Humans cause others to suffer.

Ecclesiastes 9:11
Sometimes people suffer because they are at the wrong place at the wrong time.

1 Peter 5:7
Jehovah has deep love for people. He hates to see them suffer.

TRUTH 2 — SATAN CHALLENGED JEHOVAH'S RIGHT TO RULE

"God knows that . . . your eyes will be opened and you will be like God, knowing good and bad."
—Genesis 3:5

Why did Jehovah not ignore Satan's challenge?

Genesis 3:2-5
Satan accused God of being a bad ruler. Satan wanted humans to believe that they had the right to decide for themselves what was right or wrong.

Job 38:7
Satan challenged Jehovah in front of millions of angels.

TRUTH 3

SATAN'S CHALLENGE HAS FAILED

"It does not belong to man who is walking even to direct his step."—Jeremiah 10:23

Why have humans suffered for so long?

Isaiah 55:9
Humans have had many kinds of governments, but they cannot rule the earth successfully without God.

2 Peter 3:9, 10
Jehovah is patient and has allowed time for us to come to know him and to choose him as our Ruler.

1 John 3:8
Jehovah will use Jesus to undo all the damage that Satan has done.

TRUTH 4

USE YOUR FREE WILL TO SERVE JEHOVAH

"Be wise, my son, . . . so that I can make a reply to him who taunts me."—Proverbs 27:11

Why doesn't Jehovah force us to serve him?

Proverbs 30:24
Animals act primarily because of instinct, but Jehovah has given us free will. We can decide whether we will serve him or not.

Matthew 22:37, 38
Jehovah wants us to serve him because we love him.

CHAPTER TWELVE

HOW CAN YOU BECOME GOD'S FRIEND?

WHOM do you want as your friend? Someone whom you like. Someone whom you get along with and who gets along with you. Someone who has a kind personality and qualities you admire.

2 Jehovah God selects some humans to be his friends. For example, Abraham was one of Jehovah's friends. (Isaiah 41:8; James 2:23) Jehovah also liked David. He said that David was 'a man agreeable to his heart.' (Acts 13:22) And the prophet Daniel was "very precious" to Jehovah.—Daniel 9:23.

3 How did Abraham, David, and Daniel become Jehovah's friends? Jehovah said to Abraham: "You have listened to my voice." (Genesis 22:18) Jehovah becomes a friend of those who humbly obey him. Even a nation of people could become his friends. Jehovah explained to the nation of Israel: "Obey my voice, and I will become your God, and you will become my people." (Jeremiah 7:23) So you too need to obey Jehovah if you really want to become his friend.

JEHOVAH PROTECTS HIS FRIENDS

4 The Bible says that Jehovah is looking for ways "to show his strength in behalf of those whose heart

---

1, 2. Who were some of Jehovah's friends?
3. Why were Abraham, David, and Daniel friends of Jehovah?
4, 5. How does Jehovah protect his friends?

is complete toward him." (2 Chronicles 16:9) At Psalm 32:8, Jehovah promises his friends: "I will give you insight and instruct you in the way you should go. I will give you advice with my eye upon you."

⁵ A powerful enemy wants to stop us from being God's friends. But Jehovah wants to protect us. **(Read Psalm 55:22.)** As friends of Jehovah, we serve him with all our heart. We are loyal to him even under difficult circumstances. And we have the same confidence that the psalmist had. He wrote about Jehovah: "Because he is at my right hand, I will never be shaken." (Psalm 16:8; 63:8) How does Satan try to stop us from being God's friends?

SATAN'S ACCUSATION

⁶ In Chapter 11 we learned that Satan challenged Jehovah and accused him of being a liar and of being unfair by not allowing Adam and Eve to decide for themselves what was right and what was wrong. The Bible book of Job teaches us that Satan also accuses humans who want to be friends of God. Satan claims that they serve God because of what they can get from Him, not because they love Him. Satan even claims that he can turn **anyone** against God. Let's see what we can learn from Job and how Jehovah protected him.

⁷ Who was Job? He was a good man who lived about 3,600 years ago. Jehovah said that at that time there was no man like him on the earth. Job had deep

---

6. What did Satan claim about humans?
7, 8. (a) How did Jehovah feel about Job? (b) What did Satan say about Job?

respect for God, and he hated what was bad. (Job 1:8) Yes, Job was a real friend of Jehovah.

8 Satan claimed that Job served God for selfish reasons. Satan said to Jehovah: "Have you not put up a protective hedge [or, fence] around him and his house and everything he has? You have blessed the work of his hands, and his livestock has spread out in the land. But, for a change, stretch out your hand and strike everything he has, and he will surely curse you to your very face."—Job 1:10, 11.

9 Satan accused Job of serving Jehovah only for what he could get from Him. Satan also claimed that he could get Job to stop serving Jehovah. Jehovah didn't agree with Satan, but He gave Satan permission to test whether Job was a friend of Jehovah because he loved Him.

SATAN ATTACKS JOB

10 First, Satan stole or destroyed all the animals belonging to Job. Then Satan killed most of Job's servants. Job lost everything. In a final attack, Satan killed Job's ten children in a storm. But Job remained loyal to Jehovah. "In all of this, Job did not sin or accuse God of doing anything wrong."—Job 1:12-19, 22.

11 Satan did not give up. He challenged God by saying: "Strike his bone and flesh, and he will surely curse you to your very face." So Satan struck Job with a very painful disease. (Job 2:5, 7) Again, Job was

---

9. What did Jehovah allow Satan to do?
10. How did Satan attack Job, and how did Job react?
11. (a) What else did Satan do to Job? (b) How did Job react?

loyal to Jehovah. He said: "Until I die, I will not renounce [or, give up] my integrity!"—Job 27:5.

12 Job didn't know anything about Satan's accusations or why he was suffering so much. He thought that Jehovah was the cause of his troubles. (Job 6:4; 16:11-14) But even so, Job stayed loyal to Jehovah. Now there was no doubt. Job was not selfish. He was God's friend because he loved Him. Satan's accusations were all lies!

13 Even though Job did not know what was happening in heaven, he was loyal to God and proved that Satan was evil. Jehovah rewarded Job for his loyal friendship.—Job 42:12-17.

HOW SATAN ACCUSES YOU

14 You can learn important lessons from what happened to Job. Today, Satan accuses us of serving Jehovah for what we can get from Him. At Job 2:4, Satan claimed: "**A man** will give everything that he has for his life." So Satan accuses **all** men and women of being selfish, not just Job. Hundreds of years after Job died, Satan was still insulting Jehovah and accusing his servants. For example, at Proverbs 27:11, we read: "Be wise, my son, and make my heart rejoice, so that I can make a reply to him who taunts [or, insults] me."

15 You can choose to obey Jehovah and be His loyal friend, proving that Satan is a liar. Even if you need to make big changes in your life to become God's friend, it is the best decision you could ever make!

---

12. How did Job prove that Satan was a liar?
13. What was the result of Job's loyalty?
14, 15. What is Satan's accusation against all men and women?

Jehovah rewarded Job
for his loyal friendship

This decision is a serious matter. Satan claims that **you** will not be loyal to God when you have problems. He tries to trick us into being disloyal to God. How so?

16 Satan uses many different methods to try to stop us from being God's friend. He attacks "like a roaring lion, seeking to devour someone." (1 Peter 5:8) Do not be surprised when your friends, family members, or others try to stop you from studying the Bible and from doing what is right. You may feel as if you are being attacked.* (John 15:19, 20) Satan also disguises himself "as an angel of light." So he may try to trick us into disobeying Jehovah. (2 Corinthians 11: 14) Another method Satan uses to try to stop us from serving Jehovah is to make us think that we are never good enough to serve God.—Proverbs 24:10.

OBEY JEHOVAH'S COMMANDMENTS

17 When we obey Jehovah, we prove that Satan is a liar. What will help us to be obedient? The Bible says: "You must love Jehovah your God with all your heart and all your soul and all your strength." (Deuteronomy 6:5) We obey Jehovah because we love him. As our love for Jehovah grows, we will want to do

---

* This doesn't mean that Satan is controlling the people who try to stop you from studying the Bible. But Satan is "the god of this system of things," and "the whole world is lying in [his] power." So it is not surprising when some people try to stop us from serving Jehovah.—2 Corinthians 4:4; 1 John 5:19.

---

16. (a) What methods does Satan use to try to stop people from serving Jehovah? (b) How might the Devil try to stop you personally from serving Jehovah?
17. Why do we obey Jehovah?

everything he asks us to do. The apostle John wrote: "This is what the love of God means, that we observe his commandments; and yet his commandments are not burdensome."—1 John 5:3.

18 But what are some things that Jehovah tells us are wrong? There are some examples in the box "Hate What Jehovah Hates." At first, you might think that some of these things are not so bad. But when you read the Bible verses and carefully think about them, you will understand the wisdom of obeying Jehovah's laws. You may also feel that you need to make some changes in your life. Even though this may be difficult at times, if you make those changes, you will

18, 19. (a) What are some things that Jehovah says are wrong? (b) How do we know that Jehovah isn't asking us to do something that we cannot do?

HATE WHAT JEHOVAH HATES

- **Murder**
  Exodus 20:13; 21:22, 23

- **Sexual immorality**
  Leviticus 20:10, 13, 15, 16;
  Romans 1:24, 26, 27, 32;
  1 Corinthians 6:9, 10

- **Demonism**
  Deuteronomy 18:9-13;
  1 Corinthians 10:21, 22;
  Galatians 5:20, 21

- **Idolatry**
  1 Corinthians 10:14

- **Drunkenness**
  1 Corinthians 5:11

- **Stealing**
  Leviticus 6:2, 4;
  Ephesians 4:28

- **Lying**
  Proverbs 6:16, 19;
  Colossians 3:9;
  Revelation 22:15

- **Greed**
  1 Corinthians 5:11

have the peace and happiness that come from being a loyal friend of God. (Isaiah 48:17, 18) How do we know that it is possible to make these changes?

19 Jehovah never asks us to do anything that we cannot do. (Deuteronomy 30:11-14) As a real Friend, he knows us better than we know ourselves. He knows our strengths and our weaknesses. (Psalm 103: 14) The apostle Paul encourages us: "God is faithful, and he will not let you be tempted beyond what you can bear, but along with the temptation he will also make the way out so that you may be able to endure it." (1 Corinthians 10:13) We can be confident that Jehovah will always give us the strength to do what is right. He will give you "the power beyond what is normal" to help you to endure difficult situations. (2 Corinthians 4:7) After experiencing

- **Violence**
  Psalm 11:5; Proverbs 22:24, 25; Malachi 2:16; Galatians 5:20, 21

- **Bad language and gossip**
  Leviticus 19:16; Ephesians 5:4; Colossians 3:8

- **Wrong use of blood**
  Genesis 9:4; Acts 15:20, 28, 29

- **Refusal to provide for your family**
  1 Timothy 5:8

- **Getting involved in wars or politics**
  Isaiah 2:4; John 6:15; 17:16

- **Smoking and drug abuse**
  Mark 15:23; 2 Corinthians 7:1

Jehovah's help during such times, Paul could say: "For all things I have the strength through the one who gives me power."—Philippians 4:13.

LEARN TO LOVE WHAT GOD LOVES

20 If we want to be Jehovah's friend, we must stop doing what Jehovah says is wrong, but we must also do more. (Romans 12:9) God's friends love what he loves. They are described at **Psalm 15:1-5. (Read.)** Jehovah's friends imitate his qualities and show "love, joy, peace, patience, kindness, goodness, faith, mildness, self-control."—Galatians 5:22, 23.

21 How can you learn to show those beautiful qualities? You need to learn what Jehovah loves by reading and studying the Bible regularly. (Isaiah 30:20, 21) As you do this, your love for Jehovah will grow, and as your love for him grows, you will want to obey him.

22 The changes that you may need to make in your life can be compared to taking off old clothes and putting on new ones. The Bible says that you need to "strip off the old personality" and clothe yourself with "the new personality." (Colossians 3:9, 10) Even though it may not be easy, when we make these changes and obey Jehovah, he promises to give us "a large reward." (Psalm 19:11) Yes, choose to obey Jehovah and prove that Satan is a liar. Serve Jehovah, not because of any future reward, but because of unselfish love. Then you will become a real friend of God!

---

20. What qualities should you imitate, and why?
21. How can you learn to show the qualities that God loves?
22. What will be the result if you obey Jehovah?

SUMMARY

TRUTH 1 — JEHOVAH'S FRIENDS OBEY HIM

"Obey my voice, and I will become your God, and you will become my people."—Jeremiah 7:23

Is it possible to become God's friend?

Genesis 22:18; James 2:23
Abraham became Jehovah's friend because he listened to God and put faith in Him.

2 Chronicles 16:9
Jehovah will help those who are obedient.

Psalm 25:14; 32:8
Jehovah gives insight to his friends.

Psalm 55:22
Jehovah will support his friends.

TRUTH 2 — JOB WAS GOD'S FRIEND AND STAYED FAITHFUL

"In all of this, Job did not sin or accuse God of doing anything wrong."—Job 1:22

How did Satan attack Job, and how did Job react?

Job 1:10, 11
Satan claimed that Job was selfish and did not love God.

Job 1:12-19; 2:7
Jehovah allowed Satan to take everything away from Job, and Satan even struck Job with a terrible disease.

Job 27:5
Job did not know why he was suffering so much, but he stayed faithful.

TRUTH 3   SATAN TRIES TO TURN YOU AWAY FROM JEHOVAH

"A man will give everything that he has for his life."—Job 2:4

How does Satan try to destroy our friendship with Jehovah?

2 Corinthians 11:14
Satan tries to trick us into disobeying Jehovah.

Proverbs 24:10
He tries to make us feel that we are not good enough to serve Jehovah.

1 Peter 5:8
Satan persecutes us.

Proverbs 27:11
Choose to obey Jehovah and be his loyal friend. This will prove that Satan is a liar.

TRUTH 4   WE OBEY JEHOVAH BECAUSE WE LOVE HIM

"This is what the love of God means, that we observe his commandments."—1 John 5:3

How can you become Jehovah's friend?

Deuteronomy 6:5
Show love for God. This will help you to be obedient.

Isaiah 48:17, 18
Obey Jehovah, and you will always benefit.

Deuteronomy 30:11-14
Trust that Jehovah will never ask you to do something you cannot do.

Philippians 4:13
Do what is right, and Jehovah will give you the strength you need.

CHAPTER THIRTEEN

RESPECT THE GIFT OF LIFE

JEHOVAH "is the living God." (Jeremiah 10:10) He is our Creator, and he has given us life. The Bible says: "You created all things, and because of your will they came into existence and were created." (Revelation 4: 11) Yes, Jehovah wanted us to have life. Life is a precious gift from him.—**Read Psalm 36:9.**

2 Jehovah gives us what we need to keep living, such as food and water. (Acts 17:28) But more than that, he wants us to enjoy life. (Acts 14:15-17) To be successful in life, we need to obey God's laws.—Isaiah 48:17, 18.

HOW GOD FEELS ABOUT LIFE

3 The Bible teaches us that our life and the lives of other people are precious to Jehovah. For example, when Cain—Adam and Eve's son—was very angry with his younger brother Abel, Jehovah warned Cain that he needed to control his anger. But Cain didn't listen, and he became so angry that he "assaulted his brother Abel and killed him." (Genesis 4:3-8) Jehovah punished Cain for murdering Abel. (Genesis 4:9-11) So anger and hatred are dangerous because they can make us become violent or cruel. A person who is like that cannot have everlasting life. **(Read 1 John**

1. Who gave us life?
2. How can we make a success of our life?
3. What did Jehovah do when Cain killed Abel?

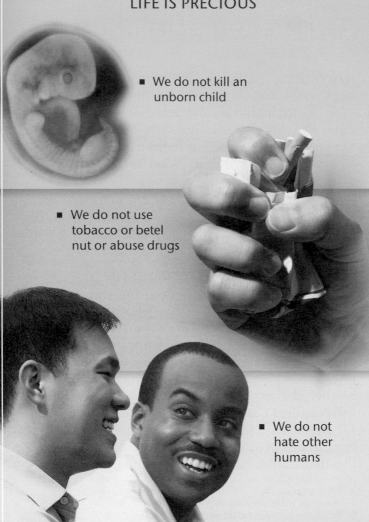

LIFE IS PRECIOUS

- We do not kill an unborn child

- We do not use tobacco or betel nut or abuse drugs

- We do not hate other humans

3:15.) To please Jehovah, we must learn to love all people.—1 John 3:11, 12.

⁴ Thousands of years later, Jehovah showed that he viewed life as precious when he gave the Ten Commandments to Moses. One of the laws is: "You must not murder." (Deuteronomy 5:17) If a person killed someone on purpose, he or she would be killed.

⁵ How does God feel about abortion? Even the life of an unborn child is precious to Jehovah. In the Law Jehovah gave to the Israelites, Jehovah said that if someone injured a mother and her baby died because of this, the person would be killed. **(Read Exodus 21: 22, 23;** Psalm 127:3.) This teaches us that abortion is wrong.—See Endnote 28.

⁶ How can we show Jehovah that we view our own life and the lives of others as precious? By not doing anything that will endanger our life or other people's lives. So we will not use tobacco or betel nut or abuse drugs, because they harm us and may kill us.

⁷ God gave us our life and our body, and we should use them as he wants us to. So we need to take good care of our body. If we don't, we will become unclean in God's eyes. (Romans 6:19; 12:1; 2 Corinthians 7:1) We cannot worship Jehovah, who gave us life, if we do not view life as precious. Even though it may be very hard to stop bad habits, Jehovah will help us if we are making the effort because we view life as precious.

---

4. What does one of the laws God gave to the Israelites teach us about the gift of life?
5. How does God feel about abortion?
6, 7. How do we show Jehovah that we view life as precious?

8 We have learned that life is a precious gift. Jehovah trusts that we will do our best never to endanger our own life or the lives of others. We do this by the way we drive our car, motorbike, or other vehicle. We avoid dangerous or violent sports. (Psalm 11:5) We also do our best to make our home safe. Jehovah commanded the Israelites: "If you build a new house, you must also make a parapet [or, low wall] for your roof, so that you may not bring bloodguilt on your house because of someone falling from it." —Deuteronomy 22:8.

9 Even the way we treat animals is important to Jehovah. He allows us to kill animals for food and for clothing, and he permits us to kill an animal if it threatens our life. (Genesis 3:21; 9:3; Exodus 21:28) But we cannot be cruel to animals or kill them just for sport.—Proverbs 12:10.

RESPECT THE HOLINESS OF LIFE

10 Blood is holy to Jehovah because blood represents life. After Cain murdered Abel, Jehovah told Cain: "Your brother's blood is crying out to me from the ground." (Genesis 4:10) Abel's blood represented his life, and Jehovah punished Cain for killing Abel. After the Flood of Noah's day, Jehovah again showed that blood represents life. Jehovah gave Noah and his family permission to eat the flesh of animals. He said:

---

8. What will we do to make sure that we don't endanger our own life or the lives of others?
9. How should we treat animals?
10. How do we know that blood represents life?

"Every moving animal that is alive may serve as food for you. Just as I gave you the green vegetation, I give them all to you." However, there was one thing that Jehovah commanded them not to eat: "Only flesh with its life—its blood—you must not eat."—Genesis 1:29; 9:3, 4.

11 About 800 years after Jehovah told Noah not to eat blood, he again commanded his people: "If one of the Israelites or some foreigner who is residing in your midst is hunting and catches a wild animal or a bird that may be eaten, he must pour its blood out and cover it with dust." He then said: "You must not eat the blood." (Leviticus 17:13, 14) Jehovah still wanted his people to view blood as holy. They could eat meat but not the blood. When they killed an animal for food, they had to pour its blood onto the ground.

12 Some years after Jesus' death, the apostles and the elders in the Christian congregation in Jerusalem met to decide what parts of the Law given to the Israelites still applied to Christians. **(Read Acts 15:28, 29; 21:25.)** Jehovah helped them to understand that blood was still precious to him and that they still needed to view it as holy. The early Christians could not eat or drink blood or eat meat that had not been bled properly. If they did so, it was just as bad as worshipping idols or being sexually immoral. From that

---

11. What command about blood did God give to the nation of Israel?
12. How do Christians view blood?

time onward, true Christians have refused to eat or drink blood. What about today? Jehovah still wants us to view blood as holy.

¹³ Does this mean that Christians should also refuse blood transfusions? Yes, it does. Jehovah commanded us not to eat or drink blood. If a doctor told you not to drink alcohol, would you inject it into your body? Of course not! In the same way, the command not to eat or drink blood means that we would not accept a blood transfusion.—See Endnote 29.

¹⁴ What if a doctor tells us that we will die if we do not have a blood transfusion? Each person must decide whether to obey God's law on blood. Christians deeply respect God's gift of life, and we will look for alternative treatments to keep living; but we will not accept a blood transfusion.

¹⁵ We try hard to keep healthy, but because life is precious to God, we will not accept a blood transfusion. It is more important to obey Jehovah than to try to extend our life by disobeying him. Jesus said: "Whoever wants to save his life will lose it, but whoever loses his life for my sake will find it." (Matthew 16:25) We want to obey Jehovah because we love him. He knows what is best for us, and we view life as precious and holy, as Jehovah does.—Hebrews 11:6.

¹⁶ God's faithful servants are determined to obey

13. Why do Christians not accept blood transfusions?
14, 15. How important is it for a Christian to respect life and obey Jehovah?
16. Why do God's servants obey him?

his law about blood. They will not eat or drink blood, and they will not accept blood for medical reasons.* However, they will accept other treatments in order to save their life. They are convinced that the Creator of life and blood knows what is best for them. Do you believe that he knows what is best for you?

THE ONLY USE OF BLOOD
THAT JEHOVAH ALLOWED

17 In the Law that God gave to Moses, Jehovah told the Israelites: "The life of the flesh is in the blood, and I myself have given it on the altar for you to make atonement [or, ask for forgiveness] for yourselves, because it is the blood that makes atonement." (Leviticus 17:11) When the Israelites sinned, they could ask for Jehovah's forgiveness by sacrificing an animal and asking the priest to pour some of its blood on the altar at the temple. This was the only way Jehovah allowed the Israelites to use blood.

18 When Jesus came to earth, he replaced the law on animal sacrifices by giving his life, or blood, for the forgiveness of our sins. (Matthew 20:28; Hebrews 10:1) Jesus' life was so valuable that after Jehovah resurrected Jesus to heaven, Jehovah could give all humans the opportunity to live forever.—John 3:16; Hebrews 9:11, 12; 1 Peter 1:18, 19.

---

* For information about blood transfusions, see pages 77-79 of the book *"Keep Yourselves in God's Love,"* published by Jehovah's Witnesses.

---

17. In Israel, what was the only use of blood that Jehovah allowed?
18. What does Jesus' sacrifice make possible for us?

How can you show respect for life and blood?

19 We are grateful to Jehovah for his wonderful gift of life! And we want to tell people that if they have faith in Jesus, they can live forever. We love people, and we will do everything we can to teach them how to get life. (Ezekiel 3:17-21) Then, like the apostle Paul, we will be able to say: "I am clean from the blood of all men, for I have not held back from telling you all the counsel of God." (Acts 20:26, 27) Yes, we show that we deeply respect life and blood when we tell others about Jehovah and how precious life is to him.

---

19. What must we do to be "clean from the blood of all men"?

TRUTH 1 — RESPECT THE GIFT OF LIFE

"With you is the source of life."—Psalm 36:9

How do we show respect for life?

Acts 17:28; Revelation 4:11
Life is a gift from Jehovah, and we should treat it with respect.

Exodus 21:22, 23; Deuteronomy 5:17
Murder and abortion are wrong.

1 John 3:11, 12, 15
Hatred is wrong.

2 Corinthians 7:1
Avoid unclean habits, such as smoking and drug abuse.

Psalm 11:5
Avoid violent entertainment and sports.

TRUTH 2 — LIFE AND BLOOD

"For the life of every sort of flesh is its blood, because the life is in it."—Leviticus 17:14

What is God's view of life and blood?

Genesis 4:10; Deuteronomy 12:23
Blood represents life.

Genesis 9:3, 4
We may eat meat but not blood.

Acts 15:28, 29; 21:25
God's command to abstain from blood includes blood used in medical treatment.

Hebrews 11:6
Our relationship with Jehovah is the most important thing in our life.

TRUTH 3

THE USES OF BLOOD JEHOVAH ALLOWED

"The blood of Jesus . . . cleanses us from all sin."—1 John 1:7

What does Jesus' sacrifice make possible for us?

Leviticus 17:11
In Bible times, when the Israelites sinned, they could ask for Jehovah's forgiveness by sacrificing an animal and asking the priest to pour some of its blood on the altar.

**Matthew 20:28;
Hebrews 9:11-14**
When Jesus came to earth, he replaced the law on animal sacrifices by giving his life, or blood, for the forgiveness of our sins.

John 3:16
Jesus' life was so valuable that after Jehovah resurrected Jesus to heaven, Jehovah gave all humans who exercise faith in Jesus the opportunity to live forever.

CHAPTER FOURTEEN

YOUR FAMILY CAN BE HAPPY

JEHOVAH GOD performed the first marriage. The Bible tells us that he made the first woman and "brought her to the man." Adam was so happy that he said: "This is at last bone of my bones and flesh of my flesh." (Genesis 2:22, 23) This tells us that Jehovah wants married people to be happy.

² Sadly, many people have never experienced a happy family life. However, the Bible contains many principles that will help all members of the family to make their family life successful and to enjoy being together.—Luke 11:28.

WHAT GOD EXPECTS FROM HUSBANDS

³ The Bible says that a good husband should treat his wife with love and respect. Please **read Ephesians 5:25-29.** A husband will always treat his wife in a loving way. He will also protect her, look after her, and do nothing that would harm her.

⁴ But what should a husband do when his wife makes mistakes? Husbands are told: "**Keep on** loving your wives and do not be bitterly angry with them." (Colossians 3:19) Husbands, remember that you too make mistakes. And if you want God to forgive you, you must forgive your wife. (Matthew 6:12, 14, 15)

1, 2. What does Jehovah want for families?
3, 4. (a) How should a husband treat his wife? (b) Why is it important for a husband and wife to forgive each other?

When a husband and wife are both willing to forgive, it will help them to have a happy marriage.

5 Jehovah expects a husband to honor his wife. A husband should think carefully about his wife's needs. This is a very serious matter. If a husband does not treat his wife well, Jehovah may refuse to listen to his prayers. (1 Peter 3:7) What makes people valuable to Jehovah is that they love him. He does not prefer men over women.

6 Jesus explained that a husband and wife "are no longer two, but **one flesh**." (Matthew 19:6) They are loyal to each other and would never be unfaithful to each other. (Proverbs 5:15-21; Hebrews 13:4) Husbands and wives should unselfishly care for each other's sexual needs. (1 Corinthians 7:3-5) A husband should remember that "no man ever hated his **own body, but he feeds and cherishes it**." So he should love and cherish his wife. More than anything else, a wife wants her husband to be kind and loving to her. —Ephesians 5:29.

WHAT GOD EXPECTS
FROM WIVES

7 Every family needs a head, someone to guide the family so that they work well together. The Bible says at 1 Corinthians 11:3: "The head of every man is the Christ; in turn, the head of a woman is the man; in turn, the head of the Christ is God."

---

5. Why should a husband honor his wife?
6. What does it mean for a husband and wife to be "one flesh"?
7. Why does a family need a family head?

How is Sarah a good example for wives?

8 Every husband makes mistakes. But when a wife supports her husband's decisions and cooperates with him willingly, the whole family benefits. (1 Peter 3:1-6) The Bible says: "The wife should have deep respect for her husband." (Ephesians 5:33) What if a husband does not share his wife's beliefs? She still needs to have deep respect for him. The Bible says: "You wives, be in subjection to your husbands, so that if any are not obedient to the word, they may be won without a word through the conduct of their wives, because of having been eyewitnesses of your chaste conduct together with **deep respect.**" (1 Peter 3:1, 2) A wife's good example can help her husband to understand and respect her faith.

9 What can a wife do when she disagrees with her husband? She should express her opinions in a

---

8. How can a wife show deep respect for her husband?
9. (a) What should a wife do if she disagrees with her husband?
(b) What is the advice for wives at Titus 2:4, 5?

respectful way. For example, Sarah said something that Abraham did not like, but Jehovah told him: "Listen to her." (Genesis 21:9-12) Rarely will a Christian husband's final decision be against what the Bible says, so his wife should support him. (Acts 5:29; Ephesians 5:24) A good wife will take care of the family. **(Read Titus 2:4, 5.)** When her husband and children see how hard she works for them, they will love and respect her even more.—Proverbs 31:10, 28.

10 Sometimes couples quickly decide to separate or divorce. However, the Bible says that "a wife should not separate from her husband" and that "a husband should not leave his wife." (1 Corinthians 7:10, 11) There are certain extreme circumstances when couples may separate, but this is a serious decision. What about divorce? The Bible shows that the only valid reason for divorce is if a husband or a wife has sex with someone other than his or her mate.—Matthew 19:9.

WHAT GOD EXPECTS FROM PARENTS

11 Parents, spend as much time as possible with your children. Your children need you, and more than anything else, they need you to teach them about Jehovah.—Deuteronomy 6:4-9.

12 Satan's world is becoming more and more wicked, and there are some people who may want to harm our children, even sexually abuse them. Some

10. What does the Bible say about separation and divorce?
11. What do children need more than anything else?
12. What should parents do to protect their children?

parents find it difficult to talk about this subject. But parents need to warn their children about such people and teach them how to avoid them. Parents, you must protect your children.*—1 Peter 5:8.

¹³ Parents have the responsibility to teach their children how to behave. How can you teach your children? Your children need training, but correction should never be cruel or harsh. (Jeremiah 30:11)

---

* You can find more information on how to protect your children in chapter 32 of the book *Learn From the Great Teacher,* published by Jehovah's Witnesses.

---

13. How should parents teach their children?

Jesus is a good example
for each member of the family

So never discipline your children when you are angry. You do not want your words to be like "the stabs of a sword" and hurt them. (Proverbs 12:18) Teach your children to understand why they need to be obedient.—Ephesians 6:4; Hebrews 12:9-11; see Endnote 30.

WHAT GOD EXPECTS FROM CHILDREN

14 Jesus always obeyed his Father, even when it was not easy. (Luke 22:42; John 8:28, 29) Jehovah also expects children to obey their parents.—Ephesians 6: 1-3.

15 Children, even if you feel that it is hard for you to obey your parents, remember that when you are obedient, Jehovah and your parents are pleased with you.*—Proverbs 1:8; 6:20; 23:22-25.

16 The Devil can use your friends and other young people to tempt you to do what is wrong. He knows that this pressure can be very hard to resist. For example, Jacob's daughter Dinah had friends who didn't love Jehovah. This caused a lot of trouble for her and her family. (Genesis 34:1, 2) If your friends do not love Jehovah, they may tempt you to do something that Jehovah hates, which would cause a lot of pain to you, to your family, and to God. (Proverbs 17:21, 25) That is why it is very important that

---

* A child doesn't have to obey his parents if they want him to do something that is against God's law.—Acts 5:29.

14, 15. Why should children be obedient to their parents?
16. (a) How does Satan try to tempt young people to do what is bad? (b) Why is it important to choose friends who love Jehovah?

you find friends who love Jehovah.—1 Corinthians 15:33.

YOUR FAMILY CAN BE HAPPY

17 When the members of a family follow God's instructions, they avoid trouble and many problems. So if you are a husband, love your wife and treat her with love. If you are a wife, be respectful and submissive to your husband and imitate the example of the wife described at Proverbs 31:10-31. If you are a parent, teach your children to love God. (Proverbs 22:6) If you are a father, guide your family "in a fine manner." (1 Timothy 3:4, 5; 5:8) And children, obey your parents. (Colossians 3:20) Remember that each person in the family can make mistakes, so be humble and ask one another for forgiveness. Yes, the Bible contains Jehovah's guidance for every person in the family.

---

17. What responsibility does each person in a family have?

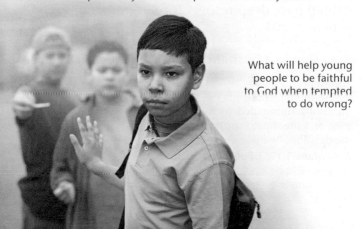

What will help young people to be faithful to God when tempted to do wrong?

TRUTH 1 — JEHOVAH CREATED THE FAMILY

"For this reason I bend my knees to the Father, to whom every family in heaven and on earth owes its name."—Ephesians 3:14, 15

How can your family be happy?

Genesis 1:26-28
Jehovah created the first family.

Ephesians 5:1, 2
The key to happy family life is imitating Jehovah and Jesus.

TRUTH 2 — HOW TO BE A GOOD HUSBAND OR WIFE

"Each one of you must love his wife . . . The wife should have deep respect for her husband."
—Ephesians 5:33

How should a husband and wife treat each other?

Ephesians 5:22-29
A husband is responsible for the family. He should love his wife, and she should support the decisions he makes.

Colossians 3:19; 1 Peter 3:4
They need to be kind and considerate to each other.

1 Peter 3:1, 2, 7
A husband and wife should honor and respect each other.

1 Timothy 5:8; Titus 2:4, 5
A husband should provide for his family. A wife should take good care of her household.

TRUTH 3 — HOW TO BE A GOOD PARENT

"Do not be irritating your children, but go on bringing them up in the discipline and admonition of Jehovah."—Ephesians 6:4

What responsibility do parents have?

**Deuteronomy 6:4-9;
Proverbs 22:6**
You need to take the time to teach your children about Jehovah. Starting when they are very young, patiently help each one to become Jehovah's friend.

1 Peter 5:8
Teach your children how they can avoid sexual abuse and other dangers.

**Jeremiah 30:11;
Hebrews 12:9-11**
You need to discipline your children but never in anger or with cruelty.

TRUTH 4 — WHAT GOD EXPECTS FROM CHILDREN

"Children, be obedient to your parents."
—Ephesians 6:1

Children, why should you be obedient to your parents?

**Proverbs 23:22-25;
Colossians 3:20**
Your obedience will make Jehovah and your parents happy.

1 Corinthians 15:33
Find friends who love Jehovah. Then it will be easier for you to do what is right.

CHAPTER FIFTEEN

THE RIGHT WAY TO WORSHIP GOD

MOST religions claim that they teach the truth about God. But that is not possible, because religions teach very different things about who God is and how we should worship him. How can we know the right way to worship God? Jehovah is the only one who can tell us how we should worship him.

2 Jehovah has given us the Bible so that we can learn the right way to worship him. So study the Bible, and Jehovah will help you to benefit from his teachings because he deeply cares for you.—Isaiah 48:17.

3 Some people say that God accepts all religions, but that's not what Jesus taught us. He said: "Not everyone saying to me, 'Lord, Lord,' will enter into the Kingdom of the heavens, but only the one doing the will of my Father." So it is necessary for us to learn what the will of God is and then to do it. This is a serious matter because Jesus compared people who do not obey God to criminals, "workers of lawlessness."—Matthew 7:21-23.

4 Jesus warned us that when we want to do the

---

1. Who should tell us the right way to worship God?
2. How can you learn the right way to worship God?
3. What does God want us to do?
4. What did Jesus say about doing God's will?

will of God, we will face challenges. He said: "Go in through the narrow gate, because broad is the gate and spacious is the road leading off into destruction, and many are going in through it; whereas narrow is the gate and cramped the road leading off into life, and few are finding it." (Matthew 7:13, 14) The cramped road, or the right way to worship God, leads to everlasting life. The spacious road, or the wrong way to worship God, leads to death. But Jehovah does not want anyone to die. He gives everyone the opportunity to learn about him.—2 Peter 3:9.

THE RIGHT WAY TO WORSHIP GOD

5 Jesus said that we can identify those who worship God in the right way. We do this by examining what they believe and what they do. He said: "By their fruits you will recognize them." And he added: "Every good tree produces fine fruit." (Matthew 7:16, 17) This doesn't mean that those who worship God are perfect. But God's servants always try to do what is right. We will now see what will help us to identify those who worship God the right way.

6 Our worship should be based on the Bible. The Bible says: "All Scripture is inspired of God and beneficial for teaching, for reproving, for setting things straight, for disciplining in righteousness, so that the man of God may be fully competent, completely equipped for every good work." (2 Timothy 3:16,

---

5. How can you identify those who worship God in the right way?
6, 7. Why is true worship based on the Bible? What does Jesus' example teach us?

17) The apostle Paul wrote to Christians: "When you received God's word, which you heard from us, you accepted it not as the word of men but, just as it truthfully is, as the word of God." (1 Thessalonians 2:13) True worship is based only on God's Word, the Bible. It is not based on human ideas, traditions, or anything else.

⁷ Everything Jesus taught was based on God's Word. **(Read John 17:17.)** He often quoted the Scriptures. (Matthew 4:4, 7, 10) True servants of God follow Jesus' example and base everything they teach on the Bible.

⁸ **We should worship only Jehovah.** Psalm 83: 18 says: "You, whose name is Jehovah, you alone are the Most High over all the earth." Jesus wanted people to know exactly who the true God is, and he taught people God's name. **(Read John 17:6.)** Jesus said: "It is Jehovah your God you must worship, and it is to him alone you must render sacred service." (Matthew 4:10) So, as God's servants, we follow Jesus' example. We worship only Jehovah, we use his name, and we teach others God's name and what he will do for us.

⁹ **We need to have genuine love for people.** Jesus taught his disciples to love one another. **(Read John 13:35.)** It doesn't matter where we're from, what our culture is, or whether we are rich or poor. Our love for one another should unite us as brothers and sisters. (Colossians 3:14) So we do not go to war and kill

---

8. What did Jesus teach us about worshipping Jehovah?
9, 10. How do we show love for one another?

people. The Bible says: "The children of God and the children of the Devil are evident by this fact: Whoever does not practice righteousness does not originate with God, nor does the one who does not love his brother." And it adds: "We should love one another; not like Cain, who originated with the wicked one and slaughtered his brother."—1 John 3:10-12; 4: 20, 21.

10 We use our time, energy, and material things to help and encourage one another. (Hebrews 10:24, 25) We "work what is good toward all."—Galatians 6:10.

11 We need to obey Jesus because he is the way to God. The Bible says: "There is no salvation in anyone else, for there is no other name under heaven that has been given among men by which we must get saved." (Acts 4:12) In Chapter 5 of this book, we learned that Jehovah sent Jesus to give his life as a ransom for obedient humans. (Matthew 20:28) Jehovah has chosen Jesus to rule as King over the earth. That is why the Bible tells us that we must obey Jesus if we want to live forever.—**Read John 3:36.**

12 We should not get involved in politics. Jesus didn't participate in politics. When he was on trial, he told the Roman ruler Pilate: "My Kingdom is no part of this world." **(Read John 18:36.)** Like Jesus, we are loyal to God's heavenly Kingdom, and for this reason, no matter where we live, we do not get involved in politics. However, the Bible commands us to obey "the superior authorities," that is,

---

11. Why do we accept Jesus as the way to God?
12. Why do we not get involved in politics?

the governments. (Romans 13:1) We obey the laws of the country where we live. Of course, when a law conflicts with God's laws, we imitate the apostles, who said: "We must obey God as ruler rather than men."—Acts 5:29; Mark 12:17.

13 We believe that God's Kingdom is the only solution for the world's problems. Jesus said that the "good news of the Kingdom" would be preached all over the world. **(Read Matthew 24:14.)** No human government can do what God's Kingdom will do for us. (Psalm 146:3) Jesus taught us to pray for God's Kingdom when he said: "Let your Kingdom come. Let your will take place, as in heaven, also on earth." (Matthew 6:10) The Bible tells us that God's Kingdom will destroy all human governments and that "it alone will stand forever."—Daniel 2:44.

14 After studying these points, ask yourself: 'Who base their teachings on the Bible? Who tell others about God's name? Who show genuine love toward one another and believe that God sent Jesus to save us? Who do not get involved in politics? Who preach that only God's Kingdom can solve our problems?' It is only Jehovah's Witnesses.—Isaiah 43:10-12.

WHAT WILL YOU DO?

15 It's not enough just to believe God exists. Even the demons believe God exists, but they don't obey him. (James 2:19) If we want God to accept our wor-

---

13. What do we preach about God's Kingdom?
14. Who do you believe worship God in the right way?
15. What must we do if we want God to accept our worship?

THOSE WHO WORSHIP GOD

- base what they teach on the Bible
- worship only Jehovah and teach others his name
- love one another
- believe that God sent Jesus to save us
- do not get involved in politics
- preach that only God's Kingdom can solve the world's problems

ship, we must not only believe he exists but also do what he says.

16 For God to accept our worship, we must reject false religion. The prophet Isaiah wrote: "Get out from the midst of her, keep yourselves clean." (Isaiah 52:11; 2 Corinthians 6:17) That is why we need to reject anything that has to do with false worship.

17 What is false religion? It is any religion that teaches us to worship God in a way that is against his Word. The Bible calls all false religion "Babylon the Great." (Revelation 17:5) Why? After the Flood of Noah's day, many false religious teachings started in the city of Babylon. Those false teachings spread all over the earth. For example, the people living in Babylon worshipped groups of three gods. Today, too, many religions teach that God is a Trinity, but the Bible clearly teaches that there is only one true God, Jehovah, and that Jesus is his Son. (John 17:3) People living in Babylon also believed that part of a person continues living after the body dies and that that part can suffer in hell. That is not true.—See Endnotes 14, 17, and 18.

18 God has foretold that soon all false religion will be destroyed. (Revelation 18:8) Do you understand why leaving false religion is so urgent? Jehovah God wants you to do that before it's too late.—Revelation 18:4.

19 When you decide to leave false religion and

---

16. Why should we reject false religion?
17, 18. What is "Babylon the Great," and why is it urgent to reject it?
19. When you decide to serve Jehovah, how will he care for you?

serve Jehovah, some of your friends or family may not understand your decision and may even make life hard for you. But Jehovah will not abandon you. You will become part of a worldwide family of millions of people who truly love one another, and you will have the hope of living forever in God's new world. (Mark 10:28-30) Perhaps some of the friends and family who oppose your decision to serve Jehovah will later decide to study the Bible.

20 Very soon, God will destroy all wickedness and his Kingdom will rule over the earth. (2 Peter 3:9, 13) That will be a wonderful time! Everyone will worship Jehovah the way Jehovah wants us to. So it's important for you to take action now and worship God in the right way.

20. Why is it important to worship God in the right way?

By serving Jehovah with his people, you will become part of a worldwide family

TRUTH 1   HOW TO RECOGNIZE TRUE WORSHIP

"Narrow is the gate and cramped the road leading off into life, and few are finding it."—Matthew 7:14

How do we know that God does not accept all kinds of worship?

Matthew 7:21-23
God does not accept all religions. Not all religions do God's will.

Matthew 7:13, 14
True worship leads to eternal life. False religion leads to eternal destruction.

Matthew 7:16, 17
You can recognize true worship by its works. You do not have to study all religions; just study what the Bible says.

TRUTH 2   THE RIGHT WAY TO WORSHIP GOD

1 Thessalonians 2:13; 2 Timothy 3:16, 17
Believe and teach only what is in the Bible.

Matthew 4:10; John 17:6
Worship Jehovah and use his name.

John 13:35
Show true love for one another.

John 3:36; Acts 4:12
Obey Jesus. God uses Jesus to save us.

John 18:36; Acts 5:29
Do not get involved in politics.

Matthew 24:14; 6:10
Teach others that God's Kingdom is the only solution to our problems.

TRUTH 3

YOU NEED TO ACT ON WHAT YOU BELIEVE

What must you do if you want God to accept your worship?

James 2:19
It is not enough just to believe in God. You need to do what he says in the Bible.

Isaiah 52:11; Revelation 17:5
False religion, or "Babylon the Great," teaches people to worship God in a way that he does not accept. False religious teachings include the Trinity, the immortality of the soul, and hellfire.

Revelation 18:4, 8
Jehovah will soon destroy all false religion. You need to reject anything that has to do with false worship.

Mark 10:28-30
You might have opposition, but Jehovah will not abandon you.

CHAPTER SIXTEEN

CHOOSE TO WORSHIP GOD

THROUGH your study of the Bible, you have learned that many people who claim to worship God actually teach or practice things that God hates. (2 Corinthians 6:17) That is why Jehovah commands us to get out of false religion, "Babylon the Great." (Revelation 18:2, 4) What will you do? Each of us has a choice to make, and we must ask ourselves, 'Do I want to worship God in the way that he wants me to, or do I want to worship him the way I always have?'

² If you have already left or resigned from a false religion, that is good. But deep inside there may be some practices and customs of false religion that you still enjoy. Let us discuss some of those practices and customs and see why it is so important that we view them the way Jehovah views them.

IMAGES AND ANCESTOR WORSHIP

³ Some people have used images or shrines in their home to worship God for many years. If that is true of you, it may feel strange or even wrong to worship God without them. But remember, Jehovah teaches us how to worship him. And the Bible clearly tells us that Jehovah does not want us to use images in our

---

1, 2. What question must you ask yourself, and why is this important?

3. (a) Why might some find it difficult to stop using images in their worship? (b) What does the Bible say about using images to worship God?

worship.—**Read Exodus 20:4, 5;** Psalm 115:4-8; Isaiah 42:8; 1 John 5:21.

4 Some people may spend a lot of time and energy trying to please their dead ancestors. They may even worship them. But we have learned that those who have died cannot help us or hurt us. They are not living somewhere else. Actually, it is dangerous to try to communicate with them because any message that appears to come from a dead relative would in fact be from the demons. That is why Jehovah commanded the Israelites not to try to talk with the dead or get involved in any other sort of demonism.—Deuteronomy 18:10-12; see Endnotes 26 and 31.

5 What can help you to stop using images to worship God or to stop worshipping your ancestors? You need to read the Bible and think carefully about how Jehovah views those things. He views them as "detestable," or disgusting. (Deuteronomy 27:15) Pray to Jehovah every day for help to view things as he does and for help to worship him in the way that he wants. (Isaiah 55:9) You can be sure that Jehovah will give you the strength you need to remove from your life anything related to false worship.

SHOULD WE CELEBRATE CHRISTMAS?

6 Around the world, Christmas is one of the most popular holidays, and most people think that it is

4. (a) Why should we not worship our ancestors? (b) Why did Jehovah tell his people not to try to speak with the dead?
5. What can help you to stop using images to worship God and to stop worshipping your ancestors?
6. Why was December 25 chosen as the day to celebrate Jesus' birth?

a celebration of the birth of Jesus. But Christmas is actually connected with false worship. One encyclopedia explains that Roman pagans celebrated the birthday of the sun on December 25. Church leaders wanted more pagans to become Christians, so even though Jesus was not born on December 25, they decided to celebrate Jesus' birth on that date. (Luke 2:8-12) Jesus' disciples did not celebrate Christmas. One reference book explains that in the 200 years after Jesus' birth, "no one knew, and few people cared, exactly when he was born." (*Sacred Origins of Profound Things*) Christmas celebrations started several hundred years after Jesus lived on earth.

7 Many people know about the pagan origins of Christmas and its traditions, such as partying and gift-giving. For example, in England and parts of America, there was a time when celebrating Christmas was forbidden because of its pagan origins. Anyone who celebrated it was punished. But eventually people began to celebrate Christmas again. Why do true Christians not celebrate Christmas? Because they want to please God in everything they do.

SHOULD WE CELEBRATE BIRTHDAYS?

8 Another popular celebration for many people is their birthday. Should Christians celebrate birthdays? The only birthday celebrations mentioned in the Bible were held by those who did not worship Jehovah. (Genesis 40:20; Mark 6:21) Birthday celebrations were used to honor false gods. That is why the early Chris-

---

7. Why do true Christians not celebrate Christmas?
8, 9. Why didn't early Christians celebrate birthdays?

tians "considered the celebration of anyone's birth to be a pagan custom."—*The World Book Encyclopedia*.

9 The ancient Romans and Greeks believed that a spirit was present at each person's birth and that this spirit would protect the person during his life. "This spirit had a mystic relation with the god on whose birthday the individual was born," explains the book *The Lore of Birthdays*.

10 Do you think that Jehovah approves of celebrations that are connected with false religion? (Isaiah 65:11, 12) No, he does not. That is why we do not celebrate birthdays or any holiday connected with false religion.

DOES IT REALLY MATTER?

11 Some people know the pagan origins of Christmas and other holidays, but they continue to celebrate them. They feel that holidays are just a good opportunity to spend time with their family. Is that how you feel? It is not wrong to want to spend time with your family. Jehovah created the family, and he wants us to have a good relationship with them. (Ephesians 3:14, 15) However, we need to focus on having a good relationship with Jehovah rather than on pleasing our relatives by celebrating false religious holidays. That is why the apostle Paul said: "Keep on making sure of what is acceptable to the Lord."—Ephesians 5:10.

12 Many people feel that where a holiday comes

---

10. Why should Christians today not celebrate birthdays?
11. Why do some people celebrate holidays? What should be most important to you?
12. What would make a holiday unacceptable to Jehovah?

from doesn't really matter, but Jehovah doesn't feel that way. He does not approve of holidays that come from false worship or that exalt humans or national symbols. For example, the Egyptians had many celebrations for their false gods. After the Israelites escaped from Egypt, they copied one of their pagan celebrations and called it "a festival to Jehovah." But Jehovah punished them for doing that. (Exodus 32: 2-10) As the prophet Isaiah said, we should "touch nothing unclean!"—**Read Isaiah 52:11.**

BE KIND WHEN DEALING WITH OTHERS

13 When you decide to stop celebrating holidays, you may have many questions. For example: What should I do if my workmates ask why I do not celebrate Christmas with them? What should I do if someone gives me a Christmas gift? What should I do if my marriage mate expects me to celebrate a holiday? How can I help my children not to feel sad because of not celebrating a holiday or their birthday?

14 It is important to use common sense when you decide what to say and do in each situation. For example, if people wish you a happy holiday, you don't need to ignore them. You can simply say, "Thank you." But in situations where someone would like to know more, you might choose to explain why you don't celebrate a holiday. However, always be kind, tactful, and respectful. The Bible says: "Let your

13. What questions may you have when you decide to stop celebrating holidays?
14, 15. What can you do if someone wishes you a happy holiday or gives you a gift?

words always be gracious, seasoned with salt, so that you will know how you should answer each person." (Colossians 4:6) Perhaps you could explain that you do enjoy spending time with others and giving gifts but that you just choose not to do so in connection with these holidays.

15 What should you do if someone gives you a gift? The Bible does not give a list of rules, but it does say that we should keep a good conscience. (1 Timothy 1: 18, 19) Maybe the person giving you the gift doesn't know that you don't celebrate a holiday. Or he might say, "I know that you don't celebrate the holiday, but I still want to give you this." In either case, you can decide if you will accept the gift or not. But whatever decision you make, be sure to keep a good conscience. We would not want to do anything that would affect our relationship with Jehovah in a bad way.

YOU AND YOUR FAMILY

16 What should you do if your family wants to celebrate a holiday? You don't have to fight with them. Remember, they have the right to decide what they want to do. Be kind and respect their choices just as you want them to respect yours. **(Read Matthew 7: 12.)** But if your family wants you to spend time with them during the holiday, what should you do? Before you decide what to do, pray to Jehovah for help to make the right decision. Think about the situation, and do research about it. Remember, you always want to please Jehovah.

---

16. What should you do if your family wants to celebrate holidays?

17 What can you do to help your children when they see others celebrating holidays? Well, from time to time, you can organize something special for them. You can also surprise them with gifts. And one of the best gifts you can give your children is your time and your love.

PRACTICE TRUE WORSHIP

18 To please Jehovah, we need to abandon false religion as well as customs and holidays related to it. But we also need to practice true worship. How? One way is by regularly attending Christian meetings. **(Read Hebrews 10:24, 25.)** The meetings are a very important part of true worship. (Psalm 22:22; 122:1) We can encourage one another when we meet together. —Romans 1:12.

19 Another part of choosing true worship is speaking to others about what you have learned from the Bible. Many people feel distressed about the wicked things happening on the earth. (Ezekiel 9:4) Maybe you know some who feel that way. Tell them about your wonderful hope for the future. As you attend Christian meetings and tell others about Bible truth, you will discover that you no longer feel the desire to be part of false religion and its customs. You can be sure that you will be happy and that Jehovah will greatly bless your efforts as you choose to worship him in the right way.—Malachi 3:10.

---

17. What can you do to help your children avoid feeling that they are missing out when others are celebrating holidays?
18. Why should we attend Christian meetings?
19. Why is it important to tell others about Bible truths you've learned?

Those who serve Jehovah
are happy

TRUTH 1   AVOID FALSE WORSHIP

"Get out from among them, and separate yourselves, . . . and quit touching the unclean thing."—2 Corinthians 6:17

Why are image and ancestor worship wrong?

Exodus 20:4, 5; 1 John 5:21
Jehovah does not want us to use images in our worship.

Deuteronomy 18:10-12
Those who communicate with the dead are actually communicating with the demons.

TRUTH 2   NOT ALL CELEBRATIONS ARE ACCEPTABLE TO GOD

"Keep on making sure of what is acceptable to the Lord."—Ephesians 5:10

How can you decide if you should participate in a celebration?

Ezekiel 44:23; 2 Corinthians 6:14, 15
Find out if it has pagan origins.

Exodus 32:2-10
Even if those initiating a celebration have good intentions, the celebration may not be approved by God.

Daniel 3:1-27
Avoid celebrations that exalt humans, human organizations, or national symbols.

1 Timothy 1:18, 19
Use common sense, but be sure to maintain a good conscience before Jehovah.

TRUTH 3

BE KIND WHEN YOU EXPLAIN YOUR BELIEFS TO OTHERS

"Let your words always be gracious, seasoned with salt, so that you will know how you should answer each person."—Colossians 4:6

How should you explain your beliefs to others?

Matthew 7:12
Respect others' choices just as you want them to respect yours.

2 Timothy 2:24
Always be kind, and do not fight with others over your beliefs.

1 Peter 3:15
Defend your beliefs with mildness and respect.

Hebrews 10:24, 25
At Christian meetings, others attending will encourage you and help you to know what to say when your beliefs are questioned.

CHAPTER SEVENTEEN

THE PRIVILEGE
OF PRAYER

COMPARED to the universe, the earth is very small. When Jehovah looks at the earth, all the people in all the nations seem like just a tiny drop of water from a bucket. (Psalm 115:15; Isaiah 40:15) Even though we are so small when compared to the universe, Psalm 145:18, 19 says: "Jehovah is near to all those calling on him, to all who call on him in truth. He satisfies the desire of those who fear him; he hears their cry for help, and he rescues them." What an amazing privilege we have! Jehovah, the almighty Creator, wants to be close to us, and he wants to listen to our prayers. Yes, prayer is a privilege, a special gift that Jehovah has given to each one of us.

² But Jehovah will listen to us only if we talk to him in the way he approves. How can we do that? Let's see what the Bible says about prayer.

WHY PRAY TO JEHOVAH?

³ Jehovah wants you to pray, or talk, to him. How do we know that? Please **read Philippians 4:6, 7.** Think about that kind invitation. The Ruler of the universe is deeply interested in you and wants you to tell him about how you feel and about your problems.

1, 2. Why do you think prayer is such a special gift, and why do we need to know what the Bible teaches about it?
3. Why should you pray to Jehovah?

"The Maker of heaven and earth" wants to hear our prayers.—Psalm 115:15

⁴ Prayer helps us to have a close friendship with Jehovah. When friends regularly talk to each other about their thoughts, concerns, and feelings, their friendship grows stronger. It's similar with prayer to Jehovah. Through the Bible, he has shared his thoughts and feelings with you, and he tells you what he will do in the future. You can share even your deepest feelings with him by talking to him regularly. As you do this, your friendship with Jehovah will grow much stronger.—James 4:8.

WHAT MUST WE DO TO BE HEARD BY GOD?

⁵ Does Jehovah listen to all prayers? No, he does not. In the time of the prophet Isaiah, Jehovah told the Israelites: "Although you offer many prayers, I am

---

4. How does regular prayer to Jehovah strengthen your friendship with him?
5. How do we know that Jehovah doesn't listen to all prayers?

not listening; your hands are filled with blood." (Isaiah 1:15) So if we are not careful, we could do things that would distance us from Jehovah, causing him to ignore our prayers.

6 If we want Jehovah to listen to our prayers, we must have faith in him. (Mark 11:24) The apostle Paul explains: "Without faith it is impossible to please God well, for whoever approaches God must believe that he is and that he becomes the rewarder of those earnestly seeking him." (Hebrews 11:6) But it is not enough just to say that we have faith. We need to prove our faith clearly by obeying Jehovah every day.—**Read James 2:26.**

7 We should be humble and respectful as we pray to Jehovah. Why? If we were to speak to a king or a president, we would do so in a respectful way. Jehovah is Almighty God, so shouldn't we show even more respect and humility when we speak to him? (Genesis 17:1; Psalm 138:6) We should also be sincere and pray to Jehovah from our heart, not just repeating the same words over and over again.—Matthew 6: 7, 8.

8 Finally, when we pray about something, we must do everything we can to work at what we are praying for. For example, if we pray to Jehovah for our daily needs, then we can't be lazy and expect Jehovah to give us everything even though we are able to work

---

6. Why is faith so important? How do you show that you have faith?
7. (a) Why should we be humble and respectful as we pray to Jehovah? (b) How can we show that we are sincere when we pray?
8. When we pray about something, what else do we need to do?

for it. We must work hard and accept whatever job we are able to do. (Matthew 6:11; 2 Thessalonians 3:10) Or if we pray to Jehovah for help to stop doing something wrong, we must avoid any situation that could tempt us. (Colossians 3:5) Let's now examine some common questions about prayer.

COMMON QUESTIONS ABOUT PRAYER

⁹ To whom should we pray? Jesus taught his followers to pray to "our Father in the heavens." (Matthew 6:9) He also said: "I am the way and the truth and the life. No one comes to the Father except through me." (John 14:6) So we should pray only **to** Jehovah **through** Jesus. What does praying through Jesus mean? For Jehovah to accept our prayers, we need to show respect for the special assignment Jehovah gave to Jesus. As we learned, Jesus came to earth to save us from sin and death. (John 3:16; Romans 5: 12) Jehovah has also appointed Jesus as High Priest and Judge.—John 5:22; Hebrews 6:20.

¹⁰ Do we need to be in a special position when we pray? No, Jehovah doesn't ask us to kneel, sit, or stand when we pray. The Bible teaches us that we can talk to Jehovah in any respectful position. (1 Chronicles 17: 16; Nehemiah 8:6; Daniel 6:10; Mark 11:25) What is most important to Jehovah is, not our position when we pray, but that we talk to him with the right attitude. We can pray out loud or silently wherever we are and at anytime during the day or night. When we pray

---

9. To whom should we pray? What does John 14:6 teach us about prayer?
10. Do we need to be in a special position when we pray? Explain.

to Jehovah, we can trust that he will hear us even when nobody else does.—Nehemiah 2:1-6.

11 What can we pray for? We can pray for anything that is acceptable to Jehovah. The Bible says: "No matter what we ask according to his will, he hears us." (1 John 5:14) Can we pray about personal things? Yes. Praying to Jehovah should be like talking to a close friend. We can tell Jehovah anything that's on our mind and in our heart. (Psalm 62:8) We can pray for him to give us his powerful holy spirit to help us do what's right. (Luke 11:13) We can also ask Jehovah for wisdom to make good decisions, and we can pray for strength to cope with difficulties. (James 1:5) We should ask Jehovah to forgive our sins. (Ephesians 1: 3, 7) We should also pray for others, including our family and our brothers and sisters in the congregation.—Acts 12:5; Colossians 4:12.

12 What should be most important in our prayers? Jehovah and his will. We should thank him from our heart for everything he has done for us. (1 Chronicles 29:10-13) We know this because when Jesus was on earth, he taught his disciples how to pray. **(Read Matthew 6:9-13.)** He said that they should first pray for God's name to be sanctified, that is, treated as sacred or holy. Then Jesus showed that we should pray for God's Kingdom to come and for Jehovah's will to be done all over the earth. It was only after praying for those very important things that Jesus said that we should pray for our personal

---

11. What are some things that we can talk to Jehovah about?
12. What should be most important in our prayers?

needs. When we put Jehovah and his will first in our prayers, we show what is most important to us.

¹³ How long should our prayers be? The Bible doesn't say. Our prayers can be short or long, depending on the situation. For example, we might say a short prayer before we eat but a longer prayer when we are giving Jehovah thanks or telling him about

---

13. How long should our prayers be?

You can pray anytime

Jehovah can answer our prayers through
the help we get from other Christians

our concerns. (1 Samuel 1:12, 15) We don't want to
say long prayers just to impress others, as some people did in Jesus' day. (Luke 20:46, 47) Jehovah is not
impressed by prayers like those. What's important to
Jehovah is that we pray from our heart.

¹⁴ How often should we pray? Jehovah invites us
to talk to him regularly. The Bible says that we should
"pray continually," "persevere in prayer," and "pray
constantly." (Matthew 26:41; Romans 12:12; 1 Thessalonians 5:17) Jehovah is always ready to listen to us.
We can thank him every day for his love and generos-
ity. We can also ask him for his guidance, strength,

---

14. How often should we pray, and what does this teach us about
Jehovah?

and comfort. If we truly value the privilege we have to pray to Jehovah, we will use every opportunity to talk to him.

15 Why should we say "amen" at the end of a prayer? The word "amen" means "surely" or "so be it." It is a way of showing that we mean what we said in our prayer, that is, that we are sincere. (Psalm 41: 13) The Bible teaches us that it is also good to say "amen," either silently or out loud, at the end of a public prayer to show that we agree with what was said.—1 Chronicles 16:36; 1 Corinthians 14:16.

HOW GOD ANSWERS OUR PRAYERS

16 Does Jehovah really answer our prayers? Yes, he does. The Bible calls him the "Hearer of prayer." (Psalm 65:2) Jehovah hears and answers the sincere prayers of millions of humans, and he does so in many different ways.

17 Jehovah uses angels and his servants on earth to provide the answer to our prayers. (Hebrews 1:13, 14) There are many examples of people who prayed for help in understanding the Bible and shortly after that received a visit from one of Jehovah's Witnesses. The Bible shows that the angels are involved in declaring "good news" all over the earth. **(Read Revelation 14:6.)** Also, many of us have prayed to Jehovah about a specific problem or need and have then

---

15. Why should we say "amen" at the end of a prayer?
16. Does Jehovah really answer our prayers? Explain.
17. How does Jehovah use angels and his servants on earth to answer our prayers?

received the help we needed from a Christian brother or sister.—Proverbs 12:25; James 2:16.

18 Jehovah uses his holy spirit to answer our prayers. When we pray for help to cope with a problem, he may use his holy spirit to give us guidance and strength. (2 Corinthians 4:7) Jehovah also uses the Bible to answer our prayers and to help us to make wise decisions. When we read the Bible, we may find scriptures that will help us. Jehovah can also motivate someone who comments at a meeting to say what we need to hear or an elder in the congregation to share a point from the Bible with us.—Galatians 6:1.

19 Sometimes, though, we might wonder, 'Why hasn't Jehovah answered my prayers yet?' Remember, he knows when and how to answer our prayers. He knows what we need. We may have to keep on praying for a time to show that we really mean what we say to him and to show him that we truly have faith in him. (Luke 11:5-10) Sometimes Jehovah answers our prayers in a way that we may not expect. For example, we may pray about a difficult situation, but instead of removing the problem, he may give us the strength to endure it.—**Read Philippians 4:13.**

20 What an amazing privilege we have to pray to Jehovah! We can be sure that he will listen to us. (Psalm 145:18) And the more often we pray to Jehovah from our heart, the stronger our friendship with him will become.

---

18. How does Jehovah use his holy spirit and the Bible to answer prayers?
19. Why might it seem that Jehovah has not answered our prayers?
20. Why should we pray to Jehovah often?

TRUTH 1

JEHOVAH WANTS TO LISTEN TO OUR PRAYERS

"Jehovah is near to all those calling on him, to all who call on him in truth."—Psalm 145:18

What should we do if we want Jehovah to listen to our prayers?

Hebrews 11:6
We must have faith.

Psalm 138:6
We must be humble and respectful.

James 2:26
Our conduct should be in harmony with our prayers.

Matthew 6:7, 8
We must be sincere and honest when we pray. We should not repeat the same words in our prayers.

Isaiah 1:15
We must live according to God's will.

TRUTH 2

COMMON QUESTIONS ABOUT PRAYER

To whom should we pray?
Matthew 6:9; John 14:6

Do we need to be in a special position to pray?
**1 Chronicles 17:16;
Nehemiah 8:5, 6;
Daniel 6:10; Mark 11:25**

Does Jehovah hear our silent prayers?
Nehemiah 2:1-6

How long should prayers be?
**1 Samuel 1:12, 15;
Luke 20:46, 47**

How often should we pray?
**Romans 12:12;
1 Thessalonians 5:17**

Why do we say "amen" at the end of a prayer?
**1 Chronicles 16:36;
1 Corinthians 14:16**

WHAT WE CAN PRAY ABOUT

"No matter what we ask according to his will, he hears us."—1 John 5:14

What are some things that we can pray for?

Matthew 6:9, 10
Pray for Jehovah's will to be done.

1 Chronicles 29:10-13
Pray to express gratitude.

Matthew 6:11-13
Pray for our personal needs and concerns.

Luke 11:13
Pray for holy spirit.

James 1:5
Pray for wisdom to make good decisions.

Philippians 4:13
Pray for strength to endure.

Ephesians 1:3, 7
Pray for forgiveness for our sins.

Acts 12:5
Pray for others.

TRUTH 4 ## JEHOVAH ANSWERS OUR PRAYERS

"O Hearer of prayer, to you people of all sorts will come."—Psalm 65:2

How does Jehovah answer our prayers?

**Proverbs 12:25;
Revelation 14:6**
Jehovah can use angels or humans to help us.

2 Corinthians 4:7
His holy spirit gives us the help we need.

Philippians 4:6, 7, 13
He gives us the peace and strength we need to endure.

**Galatians 6:1;
2 Timothy 3:16, 17**
He gives us wisdom through the Bible and the congregation.

CHAPTER EIGHTEEN

SHOULD I DEDICATE MY LIFE TO GOD AND BE BAPTIZED?

YOU have learned many Bible truths during your study of this book, such as God's promise of eternal life, the condition of the dead, and the hope of the resurrection. (Ecclesiastes 9:5; Luke 23:43; John 5:28, 29; Revelation 21:3, 4) You may have started to attend meetings of Jehovah's Witnesses and believe that they practice true worship. (John 13:35) You may have begun to develop a close friendship with Jehovah, and you may have decided that you

1. What may you think after carefully studying this book?

want to serve him. So you might think, 'What should I do now to serve God?'

2 That is what an Ethiopian man thought who lived in Jesus' time. Sometime after Jesus was resurrected, Jesus' disciple Philip preached to the man. Philip proved to him that Jesus was the Messiah. The Ethiopian man was so moved by what he learned that he immediately said: "Look! Here is water; what prevents me from getting baptized?"—Acts 8:26-36.

3 The Bible clearly teaches that if you want to serve Jehovah, you should get baptized. Jesus told his followers: "Make disciples of people of all the nations, **baptizing them.**" (Matthew 28:19) Jesus also set the example by getting baptized himself. He was completely immersed in water, not just sprinkled with water on his head. (Matthew 3:16) Today when a Christian is baptized, he must also be completely immersed, or dipped, in water.

4 When you get baptized, it shows others that you really want to be God's friend and to serve him. (Psalm 40:7, 8) So you may wonder, 'What do I need to do to get baptized?'

KNOWLEDGE AND FAITH

5 Before you can get baptized, you must **come to know** Jehovah and Jesus. You have already started

2. Why did an Ethiopian man want to get baptized?
3. (a) What command did Jesus give his followers? (b) How should a person be baptized?
4. What does your baptism show others?
5. (a) What must you do first before you can get baptized? (b) Why are Christian meetings important?

to do this by studying the Bible. (**Read John 17:3.**) But that is not enough. The Bible says that you must be "filled with the accurate knowledge" of Jehovah's will. (Colossians 1:9) The meetings of Jehovah's Witnesses will help you to have a closer relationship with Jehovah. That is one important reason for you to attend those meetings regularly.—Hebrews 10:24, 25.

6 Of course, Jehovah does not expect you to know everything in the Bible before you get baptized. He didn't expect the Ethiopian man to know everything before he got baptized. (Acts 8:30, 31) And we will continue learning about God forever. (Ecclesiastes 3:11) But to get baptized, you need to know and accept at least the basic teachings of the Bible.—Hebrews 5:12.

7 The Bible says: "Without faith it is impossible to please God." (Hebrews 11:6) So you need to have faith before you can get baptized. The Bible tells us that some people in the ancient city of Corinth heard what Jesus' followers taught and, as a result, "began to believe and be baptized." (Acts 18:8) Similarly, your study of the Bible has helped you to have **faith** in God's promises and in the power of Jesus' sacrifice, which can save us from sin and death.—Joshua 23:14; Acts 4:12; 2 Timothy 3:16, 17.

TELL OTHERS ABOUT BIBLE TRUTHS

8 As you learn more from the Bible and see how it

---

6. How much do you need to know about the Bible before you can get baptized?
7. How has your study of the Bible helped you?
8. What will motivate you to tell others about what you've learned?

helps you in your life, your faith will get stronger. You will want to **tell others about what you're learning.** (Jeremiah 20:9; 2 Corinthians 4:13) But whom should you tell?

⁹ You may want to tell your family, friends, neighbors, or workmates about what you are learning. That is good, but always do this in a kind and loving way. Eventually, you will be able to begin preaching with the congregation. When you feel ready to do so, you can talk to the Witness who is teaching you the Bible and tell him or her that you would like to share in the preaching work with the congregation. If that person thinks that you are ready and if you are living your life according to Bible standards, then together you will meet with two elders in the congregation.

¹⁰ What will happen at that meeting? The elders will talk with you to see if you understand and believe basic Bible teachings, if you obey what the Bible says in your daily life, and if you really want to become one of Jehovah's Witnesses. Remember that the elders take care of all the members of the congregation, including you, so don't be afraid to talk to them. (Acts 20:28; 1 Peter 5:2, 3) After this meeting, the elders will let you know if you can begin preaching with the congregation.

¹¹ The elders might explain to you that you need to make more changes before you can begin preaching

9, 10. (a) With whom might you begin sharing what you've learned? (b) What should you do if you want to preach with the congregation?
11. Why is it so important to make changes before you can preach with the congregation?

with the congregation. Why is it so important to make those changes? Because when we talk to others about God, we represent Jehovah and must live in a way that honors him.—1 Corinthians 6:9, 10; Galatians 5:19-21.

REPENT AND TURN AROUND

12 There is something else that you must do before you can get baptized. The apostle Peter said: "**Repent**, therefore, and turn around so as to get your sins blotted out." (Acts 3:19) What does it mean to repent? It means to feel very sorry for any wrong that we have done. For example, if you lived a sexually immoral life, then you would need to repent. And even if all your life you have tried your best to do what is right, you still need to repent, because we all sin and need to ask God for his forgiveness.—Romans 3:23; 5:12.

13 Is it enough just to feel sorry for what you have done? No. Peter said that you also need to "**turn around.**" This means that you need to reject any former wrong conduct and start doing what is right. To illustrate this, imagine that you are traveling to a certain place for the first time. After a while, you discover that you are going in the wrong direction. What would you do? No doubt you would slow down, stop, turn around, and then go in the right direction. Similarly, as you study the Bible, you might discover that there are some habits or things in your life that you need to change. Be willing to "turn around"—that is, to make the necessary changes—and begin to do what is right.

---

12. Why do all people need to repent?
13. What does it mean to "turn around"?

MAKE A PERSONAL DEDICATION

14 Another important step you need to take before getting baptized is to **dedicate** yourself to Jehovah. When you dedicate yourself to Jehovah, you say a prayer in which you promise to worship only him and to make his will the most important thing in your life.—Deuteronomy 6:15.

15 Promising to serve only Jehovah is like promising to spend the rest of your life with a person you love. Imagine that a man and a woman are dating. As the man gets to know the woman better, he comes to love her and he wants to marry her. Even though this is a serious decision, the man is willing to accept this responsibility because he loves her.

16 As you learn about Jehovah, you come to love him and want to do your best to serve him. This will motivate you to say a prayer promising to serve him. The Bible says that anyone who wants to follow Jesus must "disown himself." (Mark 8:34) What does that mean? It means that you put obedience to Jehovah first in your life. What Jehovah wants is more important than your own desires and goals.—**Read 1 Peter 4:2.**

DON'T BE AFRAID OF FAILURE

17 Some people do not dedicate themselves to Jehovah, because they are afraid that they can't keep their promise to serve him. They don't want to disappoint

14. How do you dedicate yourself to God?
15, 16. What motivates a person to dedicate himself to God?
17. Why do some people not dedicate themselves to Jehovah?

Jehovah, or they may reason that if they are not dedicated to him, then Jehovah won't hold them responsible for what they do.

18 Your love for Jehovah will help you to overcome any fear of disappointing him. Because you love him, you will do your best to keep your promise to him. (Ecclesiastes 5:4; Colossians 1:10) You will not think that it's too hard to do Jehovah's will. The apostle John wrote: "This is what the love of God means, that we observe his commandments; and yet his commandments are not burdensome."—1 John 5:3.

19 You don't have to be perfect to dedicate yourself to Jehovah. He never expects us to do more than we can do. (Psalm 103:14) He will help you to do what is right. (Isaiah 41:10) Trust in Jehovah with all your heart, and "he will make your paths straight."—Proverbs 3:5, 6.

PUBLIC DECLARATION FOR SALVATION

20 Do you think that you're ready to dedicate yourself to Jehovah? After you have dedicated yourself to Jehovah, you are ready for the next step. You need to **get baptized.**

21 Let the coordinator of the body of elders of your congregation know that you have dedicated yourself to Jehovah and that you want to be baptized. Then he

---

18. What will help you to overcome any fear of disappointing Jehovah?
19. Why shouldn't you be afraid to dedicate yourself to Jehovah?
20. After you make a personal dedication to God, what is the next step?
21, 22. How can you make a "public declaration" of your faith?

Before getting baptized, you must study the Bible

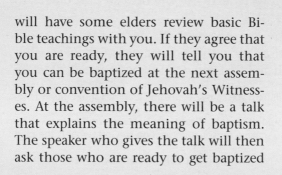

Faith should motivate you to tell others what you believe

will have some elders review basic Bible teachings with you. If they agree that you are ready, they will tell you that you can be baptized at the next assembly or convention of Jehovah's Witnesses. At the assembly, there will be a talk that explains the meaning of baptism. The speaker who gives the talk will then ask those who are ready to get baptized two simple questions. By answering those questions, you will make a "public declaration" of your faith. —Romans 10:10.

²² Then you will be baptized. You will be completely immersed in water. The baptism will show to

Have you promised Jehovah that you will serve him?

When you get baptized, you show that you want to do God's will

everyone that you have dedicated yourself to Jehovah and are now one of Jehovah's Witnesses.

WHAT YOUR BAPTISM REPRESENTS

²³ Jesus said that his disciples would be baptized "in the name of the Father and of the Son and of the holy spirit." (Read Matthew 28:19.) What does that mean? It means that you recognize Jehovah's authority and Jesus' role in God's purpose as well as how God uses his holy spirit to accomplish his will. —Psalm 83:18; Matthew 28:18; Galatians 5:22, 23; 2 Peter 1:21.

²⁴ Baptism represents something very important. When you are immersed in water, it means that you have died to, or abandoned, your former way of life. When you come out of the water, you will begin a new life doing God's will. It shows that you will serve Jehovah from now on. Remember that you are not dedicated to a human, an organization, or a work. You have dedicated your life to Jehovah.

²⁵ Your dedication will help you to develop a close friendship with God. (Psalm 25:14) This does not mean that a person will be saved just because he gets baptized. The apostle Paul wrote: "Keep working out your own salvation with fear and trembling." (Philippians 2:12) Baptism is just the beginning. But how can you stay close to Jehovah? The last chapter of this book will answer that question.

---

23. What does it mean to be baptized "in the name of the Father and of the Son and of the holy spirit"?
24, 25. (a) What does baptism represent? (b) What will we discuss in the last chapter?

TRUTH 1   SHOULD I GET BAPTIZED?

"Look! Here is water; what prevents me from getting baptized?"—Acts 8:36

Why and how should you get baptized? Baptism shows that you have abandoned your former way of life and have begun a new life doing God's will.

Matthew 28:19, 20
You need to be baptized to serve Jehovah.

Psalm 40:8
Baptism shows others that you want to serve God.

Matthew 3:16
You must be completely immersed, or dipped, under water, as Jesus was.

TRUTH 2   JEHOVAH NEVER EXPECTS TOO MUCH FROM YOU

"This is what the love of God means, that we observe his commandments; and yet his commandments are not burdensome."—1 John 5:3

Why should you not be afraid to dedicate yourself to Jehovah?

Psalm 103:14; Isaiah 41:10
You don't have to be perfect to dedicate yourself to Jehovah. He will help you to do what is right.

Colossians 1:10
Your love for Jehovah will help you to overcome your fear of disappointing him.

TRUTH 3   STEPS LEADING TO BAPTISM

"To do your will, O my God, is my delight, and your law is deep within me."—Psalm 40:8

What do you need to do to dedicate yourself to Jehovah?

John 17:3
STUDY GOD'S WORD
Come to know Jehovah and Jesus Christ. The more you learn about them, the more you will love them.

Hebrews 11:6
BUILD YOUR FAITH
Completely trust in God's promises and in the power of Jesus' sacrifice to save us from sin and death.

Acts 3:19
REPENT
This means to feel deeply sorry for all the wrong you have done.

TURN AROUND
This means to stop any wrong conduct and do what is right.

1 Peter 4:2
DEDICATE YOUR LIFE
You dedicate your life to Jehovah when you promise in prayer to worship him and to make what he wants the most important thing in your life.

CHAPTER NINETEEN

STAY CLOSE TO JEHOVAH

IMAGINE that you are walking outside on a stormy day. The sky gets darker, lightning starts to flash, and it begins to thunder. Soon the rain pours down. You search for a place to hide. What a relief when you finally find somewhere safe and dry!

² We are in a similar situation today. World conditions are getting worse. You may wonder, 'Where can I find protection?' The Bible psalmist wrote: "I will say to Jehovah: 'You are my refuge and my stronghold, my God in whom I trust.'" (Psalm 91:2) Yes, Jehovah can give us relief from our problems now, and he gives us a wonderful hope for the future.

³ How can Jehovah protect us? He can help us to deal with any problem we have, and he is far more powerful than anyone who may try to harm us. Even if something bad happens to us now, we can be sure that Jehovah will repair the damage in the future. The Bible encourages us: "Keep yourselves in God's love." (Jude 21) We need to stay close to Jehovah to receive his help during difficult times. But how can we do that?

RESPOND TO GOD'S LOVE

⁴ To stay close to Jehovah, we need to realize just

1, 2. Where can we find protection today?
3. How can we make Jehovah our refuge?
4, 5. How has Jehovah shown his love for us?

how much he loves us. Think of all that Jehovah has done for us. He has given us a beautiful earth and filled it with fascinating plants and animals. He has also given us delicious food to eat and clean water to drink. Through the Bible, Jehovah has taught us his name and his wonderful qualities. Above all, he showed his love for us when he sent his beloved Son, Jesus, to the earth to give his life for us. (John 3:16) And because of that sacrifice, we have a wonderful hope for the future.

⁵ Jehovah has provided the Messianic Kingdom, a heavenly government that will soon end all suffering. The Kingdom will make the earth a paradise, where everyone will live in peace and happiness forever. (Psalm 37:29) Another way Jehovah has shown his love for us is by teaching us how to live in the best possible way now. He also invites us to pray to him, and he is always ready to listen to our prayers. Jehovah has clearly shown his love for every one of us.

⁶ How should you respond to Jehovah's love? Show him that you are thankful for all that he has done for you. Unfortunately, many today are ungrateful. The same was true when Jesus was on earth. On one occasion, Jesus healed ten lepers, but **only one** thanked him. (Luke 17:12-17) We want to be like the man who thanked Jesus. We always want to be thankful to Jehovah.

⁷ We also need to show our love for Jehovah. Jesus told his disciples that they must love Jehovah with

---

6. How should you respond to Jehovah's love?
7. How deeply should we love Jehovah?

their whole heart, their whole soul, and their whole mind. **(Read Matthew 22:37.)** What does that mean?

8 Is it enough just to say that we love Jehovah? No. If we love Jehovah with our whole heart, soul, and mind, we will show our love for him by our actions. (Matthew 7:16-20) The Bible clearly teaches that if we love God, we will obey his commandments. Is that difficult? No, because Jehovah's "commandments are not burdensome."—**Read 1 John 5:3.**

9 When we obey Jehovah, we have a happy and satisfying life. (Isaiah 48:17, 18) But what will help us to stay close to Jehovah? Let us see.

CONTINUE DRAWING CLOSER TO JEHOVAH

10 How did you become Jehovah's friend? Through your study of the Bible, you came to know Jehovah more and developed a friendship with him. This friendship is like a fire that you want to keep burning. Just as a fire needs fuel to burn, you need to continue learning about Jehovah to keep your friendship strong.—Proverbs 2:1-5.

11 As you continue to study the Bible, you will learn things that really touch your heart. Notice how two of Jesus' disciples felt as Jesus was explaining Bible prophecies to them. They said: "Were not our hearts burning within us as he was speaking to us on the road, as he was fully opening up the Scriptures to us?"—Luke 24:32.

───

8, 9. How can we show Jehovah that we love him?
10. Why should you continue learning about Jehovah?
11. How will Bible teachings affect you?

¹² Just as the disciples' hearts were touched when they understood the Scriptures, you may have felt the same enthusiasm when you began to understand the Bible. This helped you to know Jehovah and to love him. You do not want this love to grow cold.—Matthew 24:12.

¹³ Once you become a friend of God, you need to work hard to keep your friendship strong. You must continue to learn about him and Jesus and to think about what you are learning and how you can apply it in your life. (John 17:3) When you read or study the Bible, ask yourself: 'What does this teach me about Jehovah God? Why should I love him with my whole heart and soul?'—1 Timothy 4:15.

12, 13. (a) What could happen to our love for God? (b) How can we keep our love for Jehovah alive?

Like a fire, your love for Jehovah needs fuel in order to keep burning

14 When you have a good friend, you talk to him regularly, and this keeps your friendship strong. In the same way, when we talk to Jehovah regularly in prayer, it keeps our love for him strong. **(Read 1 Thessalonians 5:17.)** Prayer is a wonderful gift from our heavenly Father. We should always speak to him from our heart. (Psalm 62:8) We should not repeat our prayers from memory, but we should really mean what we say. Yes, if we continue to study the Bible and pray from our heart, we will keep our love for Jehovah strong.

TALKING TO OTHERS ABOUT JEHOVAH

15 If we want to remain close to Jehovah, we also need to talk to others about our faith. Talking to others about Jehovah is a wonderful privilege. (Luke 1:74) And it's a responsibility that Jesus gave to all true Christians. Each of us should preach the good news of God's Kingdom. Have you already done this? —Matthew 24:14; 28:19, 20.

16 The apostle Paul felt that the preaching work was very precious; he called it a "treasure." (2 Corinthians 4:7) Telling others about Jehovah and his purpose is the most important work that you can do. It's a way for you to serve Jehovah, and he values what you do for him. (Hebrews 6:10) Preaching can also benefit both you and those who listen to you because you help others and yourself to draw close to Jehovah and to get everlasting life. **(Read 1 Corinthians**

---

14. How does prayer help keep our love for Jehovah strong?
15, 16. How do you view the preaching work?

15:58.) Is there any other work that could give you more satisfaction?

17 The preaching work is very urgent. We should "preach the word," and we should "be at it urgently." (2 Timothy 4:2) People need to hear about God's Kingdom. The Bible says: "The great day of Jehovah is near! It is near and it is approaching very quickly!" The end "will not be late!" (Zephaniah 1:14; Habakkuk 2:3) Yes, very soon, Jehovah will destroy Satan's wicked world. Before that happens, people need to be warned so that they can choose to serve Jehovah.

18 Jehovah wants us to worship him along with other true Christians. The Bible says: "Let us consider one another so as to incite to love and fine works, not forsaking our meeting together, as some have the custom, but encouraging one another, and all the more so as you see the day drawing near." (Hebrews 10:24, 25) We should do our best to be at all the meetings. The meetings give us an opportunity to encourage and strengthen one another.

19 When you attend meetings, you'll find good friends who will help you to worship Jehovah. You'll meet a variety of brothers and sisters who, like you, do their best to worship him. And like you, they're imperfect and make mistakes. When they do, be ready to forgive them. **(Read Colossians 3:13.)** Always focus on the good qualities of your Christian

17. Why is the preaching work urgent?
18. Why should we worship Jehovah along with other true Christians?
19. What can help us to love our Christian brothers and sisters?

brothers and sisters, for doing that will help you to love them and draw ever closer to Jehovah.

THE REAL LIFE

20 Jehovah wants all his friends to have the best life possible. The Bible teaches us that our life in the future will be completely different from our life today.

21 In the future, we will live forever, not just for 70 or 80 years. We will enjoy "everlasting life" in perfect health, peace, and happiness in a beautiful paradise. That is what the Bible calls "the real life." Jehovah promises to give us this real life, but we must do all we can now to get a "firm hold" on it.—1 Timothy 6: 12, 19.

22 How can we "get a firm hold on the real life"? We must "work at good" and "be rich in fine works." (1 Timothy 6:18) This means that we need to apply what we learn from the Bible. However, the real life does not depend on our own efforts. We can never earn eternal life. It's a free gift from Jehovah to his faithful servants, an example of his "undeserved kindness." (Romans 5:15) Our heavenly Father really wants to give his faithful servants this gift.

23 Ask yourself, 'Am I worshipping God the way he approves?' If you find that you need to make some changes, you should do so right away. When we rely on Jehovah and do everything we can to obey him, Jehovah will be our refuge. He will keep his faithful

---

20, 21. What is "the real life"?
22. (a) How can we "get a firm hold on the real life"? (b) Why can we not earn eternal life?
23. Why do you need to make the right choices now?

people safe during the last days of Satan's wicked world. Then Jehovah will make sure that we live in Paradise forever, just as he has promised. Yes, you can have the real life if you make the right choices now!

Jehovah wants you to enjoy "the real life." **Will you?**

TRUTH 1 — JEHOVAH LOVES YOU

"God loved the world so much that he gave his only-begotten Son, so that everyone exercising faith in him might not be destroyed but have everlasting life."—John 3:16

How does God show love for you?

Psalm 91:2
Jehovah is our refuge.
He can give us relief
from our problems now.

Psalm 37:29
He has given us a wonderful
hope for the future.

1 Timothy 6:12, 19
God will give us eternal life
in perfect conditions. We will
enjoy peace, happiness, and
perfect health in a beautiful
paradise.

TRUTH 2 — JEHOVAH WANTS YOU TO LOVE HIM

"You must love Jehovah your God with your whole heart and with your whole soul and with your whole mind."—Matthew 22:37

What does God's love motivate you to do?

Luke 17:12-17
Be thankful for everything
God has done for you.

Matthew 7:16-20
Show your love for God
by doing his will each day.

1 John 5:3
Obey God's commands.

1 Timothy 6:18
Work hard to do good
for others.

TRUTH 3

KEEP YOUR LOVE
FOR JEHOVAH STRONG

"Keep yourselves in God's love."—Jude 21

What will help you to stay close to Jehovah?

1 Thessalonians 5:17
Pray often.

**Matthew 28:19, 20;
2 Timothy 4:2**
Do all you can to talk to
others about God's Kingdom.

Proverbs 2:1-5
Keep learning about Jehovah.

Hebrews 10:24, 25
Attend meetings regularly.
Your Christian brothers and
sisters will help you to draw
even closer to Jehovah.

ENDNOTES

1   JEHOVAH

God's name is Jehovah and is understood to mean "He Causes to Become." Jehovah is the almighty God, and he created everything. He has the power to do anything he decides to do.

In Hebrew, God's name was written with four letters. In English, these are represented by YHWH or JHVH. God's name appears in the original Hebrew text of the Bible nearly 7,000 times. People all over the world use different forms of the name Jehovah, pronouncing it in the way that is common in their language.

▸ Chap. 1, par. 15

2   THE BIBLE IS "INSPIRED OF GOD"

The Author of the Bible is God, but he used men to write it. This is similar to a businessman telling his secretary to write a letter that contains his ideas. God used his holy spirit to guide the Bible writers to record his thoughts. God's spirit guided them in various ways, sometimes causing them to see visions or have dreams that they would then write down.

▸ Chap. 2, par. 5

3   PRINCIPLES

These are teachings in the Bible that explain a basic truth. For example, the principle "bad associations spoil useful habits" teaches us that we are affected for good or for bad by the people with whom we associate. (1 Corinthians 15:33) And the principle "whatever a person is sowing, this he will also reap" teaches us that we cannot escape the results of our actions.—Galatians 6:7.

▸ Chap. 2, par. 12

4 PROPHECY

This is a message from God. It could be an explanation of God's will, a moral teaching, a command, or a judgment. It can also be a message about something that will happen in the future. There are many prophecies in the Bible that have already come true.

▸ Chap. 2, par. 13

5 PROPHECIES ABOUT THE MESSIAH

Jesus is the one who fulfilled the many Bible prophecies about the Messiah. See the box "Prophecies About the Messiah."

▸ Chap. 2, par. 17, ftn.

6 JEHOVAH'S PURPOSE FOR THE EARTH

Jehovah created the earth to be a paradise home for humans who love him. His purpose has not changed. Soon, God will remove wickedness and give his people everlasting life.

▸ Chap. 3, par. 1

7 SATAN THE DEVIL

Satan is the angel who started the rebellion against God. He is called Satan, which means "Resister," because he fights against Jehovah. He is also called Devil, which means "Slanderer." This name was given to him because he tells lies about God and deceives people.

▸ Chap. 3, par. 4

PROPHECIES ABOUT THE MESSIAH

EVENT	PROPHECY	FULFILLMENT
Born of the tribe of Judah	Genesis 49:10	Luke 3:23-33
Born of a virgin	Isaiah 7:14	Matthew 1:18-25
A descendant of King David	Isaiah 9:7	Matthew 1:1, 6-17
Jehovah declared Jesus to be his Son	Psalm 2:7	Matthew 3:17
Many people did not believe that Jesus was the Messiah	Isaiah 53:1	John 12:37, 38
Entered Jerusalem riding a donkey	Zechariah 9:9	Matthew 21:1-9
Betrayed by a close friend	Psalm 41:9	John 13:18, 21-30
Betrayed for 30 silver pieces	Zechariah 11:12	Matthew 26:14-16
Silent when he was accused	Isaiah 53:7	Matthew 27:11-14
Lots were cast for his garments	Psalm 22:18	Matthew 27:35
Mocked while on the stake	Psalm 22:7, 8	Matthew 27:39-43
None of his bones broken	Psalm 34:20	John 19:33, 36
Buried with the rich	Isaiah 53:9	Matthew 27:57-60
His resurrection	Psalm 16:10	Acts 2:24, 27
Resurrected to heaven to be at God's right hand	Psalm 110:1	Acts 7:55, 56

8   ANGELS

Jehovah created the angels long before he created the earth. They were created to live in heaven. There are more than a hundred million angels. (Daniel 7:10) They have names and different personalities, and loyal angels humbly refuse to be worshipped by humans. They have different ranks and are assigned a variety of work. Some of this work includes serving before Jehovah's throne, delivering his messages, protecting and guiding his servants on earth, carrying out his judgments, and supporting the preaching work. (Psalm 34:7; Revelation 14:6; 22:8, 9) In the future, they will fight alongside Jesus in the war of Armageddon.—Revelation 16:14, 16; 19:14, 15.

▸ Chap. 3, par. 5; Chap. 10, par. 1

9   SIN

Anything that we feel, think, or do that is against Jehovah or his will is sin. Because sin damages our relationship with God, he has given us laws and principles that help us to avoid intentional sin. In the beginning, Jehovah created everything perfect, but when Adam and Eve chose to disobey Jehovah, they sinned and were no longer perfect. They grew old and died, and because we inherited sin from Adam, we too grow old and die.

▸ Chap. 3, par. 7; Chap. 5, par. 3

10   ARMAGEDDON

This is God's war to destroy Satan's world and all wickedness.

▸ Chap. 3, par. 13; Chap. 8, par. 18

11 GOD'S KINGDOM

God's Kingdom is a government that Jehovah has set up in heaven. Jesus Christ is ruling as its King. In the future, Jehovah will use the Kingdom to remove all wickedness. God's Kingdom will rule over the earth.

▸ Chap. 3, par. 14

12 JESUS CHRIST

God created Jesus before everything else. Jehovah sent Jesus to earth to die for all humans. After Jesus was killed, Jehovah resurrected him. Jesus is now ruling in heaven as King of God's Kingdom.

▸ Chap. 4, par. 2

13 THE PROPHECY OF THE 70 WEEKS

The Bible prophesied, or foretold, when the Messiah would appear. This would be at the end of a period of time called the 69 weeks, which began in the year 455 B.C.E. and ended in the year 29 C.E.

How do we know that it ended in 29 C.E.? The 69 weeks began in the year 455 B.C.E. when Nehemiah arrived in Jerusalem and began to rebuild the city. (Daniel 9:25; Nehemiah 2:1, 5-8) Just as the word "dozen" makes us think of the number 12, so the word "week" reminds us of the number 7. The weeks in this prophecy are not weeks of seven days but are weeks of seven years, in line with the prophetic rule of "a day for a year." (Numbers 14:34; Ezekiel 4:6) This means that each week is seven years long and that the 69 weeks add up to 483 years (69 x 7). If we count 483 years from 455 B.C.E., it takes us to the year 29 C.E. This is exactly the year when Jesus was baptized and became the Messiah!—Luke 3:1, 2, 21, 22.

The same prophecy foretold another week, which is an extra seven years. During this time period, in the year 33 C.E., the Messiah would be killed, and beginning in the year 36 C.E., the good news of God's Kingdom would be preached to all the nations and not just to the Jews. —Daniel 9:24-27.

▸ Chap. 4, par. 7

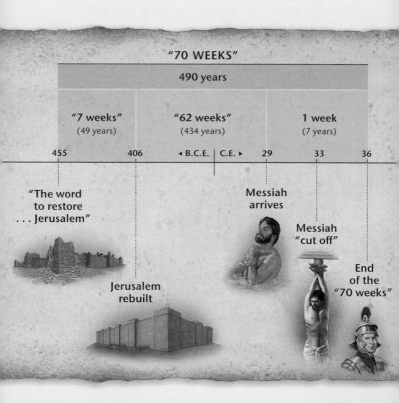

"70 WEEKS"

490 years

| "7 weeks" (49 years) | "62 weeks" (434 years) | 1 week (7 years) |

455   406   ◂ B.C.E. | C.E. ▸   29   33   36

"The word to restore . . . Jerusalem"

Messiah arrives

Messiah "cut off"

Jerusalem rebuilt

End of the "70 weeks"

14   THE FALSE TEACHING OF THE TRINITY

The Bible teaches that Jehovah God is the Creator and that he created Jesus before all other things. (Colossians 1:15, 16) Jesus is not Almighty God. He never claimed that he was equal to God. In fact, he said: "The Father is greater than I am." (John 14:28; 1 Corinthians 15:28) But some religions teach the Trinity, that God is three persons in one: the Father, the Son, and the holy spirit. The word "Trinity" is not in the Bible. This is a false teaching.

The holy spirit is God's active force, his invisible power in action that he uses to do his will. It is not a person. For example, early Christians "became *filled* with holy spirit," and Jehovah said: "I will *pour out* some of my spirit on every sort of flesh."—Acts 2:1-4, 17.

▶ Chap. 4, par. 12; Chap. 15, par. 17

15   THE CROSS

When true Christians worship God, they do not use the cross. Why not?

(1) The cross has been used in false religion for a long time. In ancient times it was used in nature worship and in pagan sex rites. During the first 300 years after Jesus' death, Christians did not use the cross in their worship. Much later, Roman Emperor Constantine made the cross a symbol of Christianity. The symbol was used to try to make Christianity more popular. But the cross had nothing to do with Jesus Christ. The *New Catholic Encyclopedia* explains: "The cross is found in both pre-Christian and non-Christian cultures."

(2) Jesus did not die on a cross. The Greek words translated "cross" basically mean "an upright stake," "a timber," or "a tree." *The Companion Bible* explains: "There is nothing in the Greek of the [New Testament]

even to imply two pieces of timber." Jesus died on an upright stake.

(3) Jehovah does not want us to use images or symbols in our worship.—Exodus 20:4, 5; 1 Corinthians 10:14.

▸ Chap. 5, par. 12

16 THE MEMORIAL

Jesus commanded his disciples to observe the Memorial of his death. They do this each year on Nisan 14, the same date that the Israelites celebrated the Passover. Bread and wine, which represent Jesus' body and blood, are passed around to everyone at the Memorial. Those who will rule with Jesus in heaven eat the bread and drink the wine. Those who have the hope of living forever on earth respectfully attend the Memorial but do not eat the bread or drink the wine.

▸ Chap. 5, par. 21

17 SOUL

In the English edition of the *New World Translation,* the word "soul" is used to describe (1) a person, (2) an animal, or (3) the life of a person or an animal. Here are some examples:

A person. "In Noah's day . . . a few people, that is, eight souls, were carried safely through the water." (1 Peter 3: 20) Here the word "souls" refers to people—Noah and his wife, their three sons, and the sons' wives.

An animal. "God said: 'Let the waters swarm with living creatures ["souls," footnote], and let flying creatures fly above the earth across the expanse of the heavens.' Then God said: 'Let the earth bring forth living creatures ["souls," footnote] according to their kinds, domestic animals and creeping animals and wild animals of the earth according to their kinds.' And it was so."—Genesis 1:20, 24.

The life of a person or an animal. Jehovah told Moses: "All the men who were seeking to kill you ["seeking your soul," footnote] are dead." (Exodus 4:19) When Jesus was on earth, he said: "I am the fine shepherd; the fine shepherd surrenders his life ["soul," footnote] in behalf of the sheep."—John 10:11.

In addition, when a person does something with his "whole soul," this means that he does it willingly and to the best of his ability. (Matthew 22:37; Deuteronomy 6:5) The word "soul" can also be used to describe the desire or appetite of a living creature. A dead person or a dead body can be referred to as a dead soul.—Numbers 6:6; Proverbs 23:2; Isaiah 56:11; Haggai 2:13.

▸ Chap. 6, par. 5; Chap. 15, par. 17

18 SPIRIT

The Hebrew and Greek words translated "spirit" in the English edition of the *New World Translation* can mean different things. Yet they always refer to something invisible to humans, such as the wind or the breath of humans and animals. These words may also refer to spirit persons and to the holy spirit, which is God's active force. The Bible does not teach that a separate part of a person keeps on living after he dies.—Exodus 35:21; Psalm 104:29; Matthew 12:43; Luke 11:13.

▸ Chap. 6, par. 5; Chap. 15, par. 17

19 GEHENNA

Gehenna is the name of a valley near Jerusalem where garbage was burned and destroyed. There is no evidence that in Jesus' time animals or humans were tortured or burned alive in this valley. So Gehenna does not symbolize an invisible place where people who have died are tortured and burned forever. When Jesus spoke of those who are thrown into Gehenna, he was talking about complete destruction.—Matthew 5:22; 10:28.

▸ Chap. 7, par. 20

20   THE LORD'S PRAYER

This is the prayer Jesus gave when teaching his disciples how to pray. It is also called the Our Father prayer or the model prayer. For example, Jesus taught us to pray this way:

"Let your name be sanctified"
We pray for Jehovah to clear his name, or reputation, of all lies. This is so that everyone in heaven and on earth will honor and respect God's name.

"Let your Kingdom come"
We pray for God's government to destroy Satan's wicked world, to rule over the earth, and to make the earth into a paradise.

"Let your will take place . . . on earth"
We pray for God's purpose for the earth to be fulfilled so that obedient, perfect humans can live forever in Paradise, just as Jehovah wanted when humans were created.

▸ Chap. 8, par. 2

21   THE RANSOM

Jehovah provided the ransom to save humans from sin and death. The ransom was the price needed to buy back the perfect human life that the first man, Adam, lost and to repair man's damaged relationship with Jehovah. God sent Jesus to earth so that he could die for all sinners. Because of Jesus' death, all humans have the opportunity to live forever and become perfect.

▸ Chap. 8, par. 21; Chap. 9, par. 13

22   WHY IS THE YEAR 1914 SO IMPORTANT?

The prophecy in Daniel chapter 4 teaches us that God would set up his Kingdom in 1914.

The prophecy: Jehovah gave King Nebuchadnezzar a prophetic dream about a large tree that was chopped down. In the dream, a band of iron and copper was put around the tree's stump to stop it from growing for a period of "seven times." After that, the tree would grow again.—Daniel 4:1, 10-16.

What the prophecy means for us: The tree represents God's rulership. For many years, Jehovah used kings in Jerusalem to rule over the nation of Israel. (1 Chronicles 29:23) But those kings became unfaithful, and their rulership ended. Jerusalem was destroyed in the year 607 B.C.E. That was the start of the "seven times." (2 Kings 25:1, 8-10; Ezekiel 21:25-27) When Jesus said, "Jerusalem will be trampled on by the nations until the appointed times of the nations are fulfilled," he was talking about the "seven times." (Luke 21:24) So the "seven times" did not end when Jesus was on earth. Jehovah promised to appoint a King at the end of the "seven times." The rulership of this new King, Jesus, would bring great blessings for God's people all over the earth, forever.—Luke 1:30-33.

The length of the "seven times": The "seven times" lasted for 2,520 years. If we count 2,520 years from the year 607 B.C.E., we end up at the year 1914. That was when Jehovah made Jesus, the Messiah, King of God's Kingdom in heaven.

NEBUCHADNEZZAR'S TREE DREAM
WHAT IT TEACHES US ABOUT GOD'S KINGDOM

THE PROPHECY

A large tree
(Daniel 4:10, 11)

"Chop down the tree"
(Daniel 4:14)

Rulership   **Rulership ends**

WHAT THE PROPHECY MEANS

Israelite kings who ruled
over God's people

Jerusalem was destroyed,
and the rule of the Israelite
kings ended

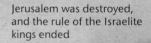

October
607 B.C.E.

"Let **seven times**
pass"
(Daniel 4:16)

"Your kingdom
will be yours again"
(Daniel 4:26)

"Seven times"

Rulership is restored

2,520 years

Jesus begins ruling
in heaven as King
of God's Kingdom

B.C.E.	C.E.	
606 1/4 years	1,913 3/4 years	October **1914 C.E.**

"Jerusalem will be
trampled on . . .
until *the appointed
times* of the nations
are fulfilled"
(Luke 21:24)

How do we get the number 2,520? The Bible says that three and a half times equal 1,260 days. (Revelation 12: 6, 14) So "seven times" is double that number, or 2,520 days. The 2,520 days are equal to 2,520 years because of the prophetic rule "a day for a year."—Numbers 14:34; Ezekiel 4:6.

▸ Chap. 8, par. 23

23 MICHAEL THE ARCHANGEL

The word "archangel" means "chief of the angels." The Bible mentions only one archangel, and his name is Michael.—Daniel 12:1; Jude 9.

Michael is the Leader of God's army of faithful angels. Revelation 12:7 says: "Michael and his angels battled with the dragon . . . and its angels." The book of Revelation says that the Leader of God's army is Jesus, so Michael is another name for Jesus.—Revelation 19:14-16.

▸ Chap. 9, par. 4

24 THE LAST DAYS

This expression refers to the time period when major events would happen on earth just before God's Kingdom destroys Satan's world. Similar expressions, such as "the conclusion of the system of things" and "the presence of the Son of man," are used in Bible prophecy to refer to the same time period. (Matthew 24:3, 27, 37) "The last days" started when God's Kingdom began ruling in heaven in 1914 and will end when Satan's world is destroyed at Armageddon.—2 Timothy 3:1; 2 Peter 3:3.

▸ Chap. 9, par. 5

25   RESURRECTION

When God brings a person who has died back to life, it is called a resurrection. Nine resurrections are mentioned in the Bible. Elijah, Elisha, Jesus, Peter, and Paul all performed resurrections. These miracles were possible only because of God's power. Jehovah promises to resurrect "both the righteous and the unrighteous" to life on earth. (Acts 24:15) The Bible also mentions a resurrection to heaven. This takes place when those who are chosen, or anointed, by God are resurrected to live in heaven with Jesus.—John 5:28, 29; 11:25; Philippians 3:11; Revelation 20:5, 6.

▸ Chap. 9, par. 13

26   DEMONISM (SPIRITISM)

Demonism or spiritism is the bad practice of trying to communicate with spirits, either directly or through someone else, such as a witch doctor, a medium, or a psychic. People who practice spiritism do this because they believe the false teaching that spirits of humans survive death and become powerful ghosts. The demons also try to influence humans to disobey God. Astrology, divination, magic, witchcraft, superstitions, the occult, and the supernatural are also part of demonism. Many books, magazines, horoscopes, movies, posters, and even songs make the demons, magic, and the supernatural seem harmless or exciting. Many funeral customs, such as sacrifices for the dead, funeral celebrations, funeral anniversaries, widowhood rites, and some wake rituals, also include contact with the demons. People often use drugs when trying to use the power of the demons. —Galatians 5:20; Revelation 21:8.

▸ Chap. 10, par. 10; Chap. 16, par. 4

27 JEHOVAH'S SOVEREIGNTY

Jehovah is Almighty God, and he created the whole universe. (Revelation 15:3) That is why he is the Owner of all things and has sovereignty, or complete authority, to rule over his creation. (Psalm 24:1; Isaiah 40:21-23; Revelation 4:11) He has made laws for everything that he has created. Jehovah also has the authority to appoint others to be rulers. We support God's sovereignty when we love him and obey him.—1 Chronicles 29:11.

▸ Chap. 11, par. 10

28 ABORTION

An abortion is done intentionally to cause the death of an unborn child. It is not an accident or the result of a natural reaction of the human body. From the time of conception, a child is not just another part of the mother's body. The child is a separate person.

▸ Chap. 13, par. 5

29 BLOOD TRANSFUSION

This is the medical procedure in which whole blood or one of its four main components is transferred into a person's body from another person or from blood that has been stored. The four main components of blood are plasma, red blood cells, white blood cells, and platelets.

▸ Chap. 13, par. 13

30 DISCIPLINE

In the Bible, the word for "discipline" is not just another word for punishment. When we are disciplined, we are instructed, educated, and corrected. Jehovah is never abusive or cruel to those he disciplines. (Proverbs 4: 1, 2) Jehovah sets a beautiful example for parents. The discipline he gives is so effective that a person can actually come to love discipline. (Proverbs 12:1) Jehovah loves his people, and he trains them. He gives them instruction that corrects wrong ideas and that helps them to learn to think and act in a way that pleases him. For parents, discipline includes helping their children to understand the reasons why they should be obedient. It also means teaching them to love Jehovah, as well as to love his Word, the Bible, and to understand its principles.

▸ Chap. 14, par. 13

31 DEMONS

They are invisible, wicked spirit creatures with superhuman powers. The demons are wicked angels. They became wicked when they made themselves enemies of God by disobeying him. (Genesis 6:2; Jude 6) They joined Satan's rebellion against Jehovah. —Deuteronomy 32:17; Luke 8:30; Acts 16:16; James 2:19.

▸ Chap. 16, par. 4

For more information, visit **www.jw.org** or contact Jehovah's Witnesses.

ALBANIA: PO Box 118, Tiranë. **ANGOLA:** Caixa Postal 6877, Luanda. **ARGENTINA:** Casilla 83 (Suc 27B), C1427WAB Cdad. Aut. de Buenos Aires. **ARMENIA:** PO Box 75, 0010 Yerevan. **AUSTRALASIA:** PO Box 280, Ingleburn, NSW 1890, Australia. **BARBADOS, W.I.:** Crusher Site Road, Prospect, BB 24012 St. James. **BELARUS:** PO Box 9, 220030 Minsk. **BELGIUM:** rue d'Argile-Potaardestraat 60, B-1950 Kraainem. **BENIN:** BP 312, AB-Calavi. **BOLIVIA:** Casilla 6397, Santa Cruz. **BRAZIL:** Rodovia SP-141, km 43, Cesário Lange, SP, 18285-901. **BRITAIN:** The Ridgeway, London NW7 1RN. **BULGARIA:** PO Box 424, 1618 Sofia. **BURUNDI:** BP 2150, Bujumbura. **CAMEROON:** BP 889, Douala. **CANADA:** PO Box 4100, Georgetown, ON L7G 4Y4. **CENTRAL AFRICAN REPUBLIC:** BP 662, Bangui. **CENTRAL AMERICA:** Apartado Postal 895, 06002 México, D.F., México. **CENTRAL EUROPE:** 65617 Selters, Germany. **CHILE:** Casilla 267, Puente Alto. **COLOMBIA:** Apartado 85058, Bogotá. **CONGO, DEMOCRATIC REPUBLIC OF:** BP 634, Limete, Kinshasa. **CÔTE D'IVOIRE:** 06 BP 393, Abidjan 06. **CROATIA:** Štrokinec 28, HR-10090 Zagreb-Susedgrad. **CZECH-SLOVAK:** PO Box 2, 830 04 Bratislava 34, Slovak Republic. **DOMINICAN REPUBLIC:** Apartado 1742, Santo Domingo. **ECUADOR:** Casilla 09-01-1334, Guayaquil. **ETHIOPIA:** PO Box 5522, Addis Ababa. **FIJI:** PO Box 23, Suva. **FINLAND:** PO Box 68, FI-01301 Vantaa. **FRANCE:** BP 625, F-27406 Louviers Cedex. **GEORGIA:** Postbox 237, Tbilisi, 0102. **GHANA:** PO Box GP 760, Accra. **GREECE:** Kifisias 77, GR 151 24 Marousi. **HAITI:** PO Box 185, Port-au-Prince. **HONG KONG:** 22/F, 1 Hung To Road, Kwun Tong. **HUNGARY:** Budapest, Pf 20, H-1631. **INDIA:** PO Box 6441, Yelahanka, Bangalore-KAR 560 064. **INDONESIA:** PO Box 11, JKB 11000. **ISRAEL:** PO Box 29 345, 61 292 02 Tel Aviv. **ITALY:** Via della Bufalotta 1281, I-00138 Rome RM. **JAPAN:** 4-7-1 Nakashinden, Ebina City, Kanagawa-Pref, 243-0496. **KAZAKHSTAN:** PO Box 198, Almaty, 050000. **KENYA:** PO Box 21290, Nairobi 00505. **KOREA, REPUBLIC OF:** PO Box 33, Pyeongtaek PO, Gyeonggi-do, 17895. **KYRGYZSTAN:** PO Box 80, 720080 Bishkek. **LIBERIA:** PO Box 10-0380, 1000 Monrovia 10. **MACEDONIA:** Pf 800, 1000 Skopje. **MADAGASCAR:** BP 116, 105 Ivato. **MALAWI:** PO Box 30749, Lilongwe 3. **MALAYSIA:** Peti Surat No. 580, 75760 Melaka. **MALTA:** IBSA House, Triq il-Waqqafa, Mosta MST 4486. **MICRONESIA:** 143 Jehovah St, Barrigada, GU 96913. **MOLDOVA, REPUBLIC OF:** PO Box 472, MD-2005 Chişinău. **MOZAMBIQUE:** PO Box 2600, 1100 Maputo. **MYANMAR:** PO Box 62, Yangon. **NEPAL:** PO Box 24438, GPO, Kathmandu. **NETHERLANDS:** Noordbargerstraat 77, 7812 AA Emmen. **NEW CALEDONIA:** BP 1741, 98874 Pont des Français. **NIGERIA:** PMB 1090, Benin City 300001, Edo State. **PAPUA NEW GUINEA:** PO Box 636, Boroko, NCD 111. **PARAGUAY:** Casilla 482, 1209 Asunción. **PERU:** Apartado 18-1055, Lima 18. **PHILIPPINES:** PO Box 2044, 1060 Manila. **POLAND:** ul. Warszawska 14, 05-830 Nadarzyn. **PORTUGAL:** Apartado 91, P-2766-955 Estoril. **ROMANIA:** CP 132, OP 39, Bucureşti. **RUSSIA:** PO Box 182, 190000 St. Petersburg. **RWANDA:** BP 529, Kigali. **SCANDINAVIA:** PO Box 340, DK-4300 Holbæk, Denmark. **SENEGAL:** BP 29896, 14523 Dakar. **SERBIA:** PO Box 173, SRB 11080 Beograd/Zemun. **SIERRA LEONE:** PO Box 136, Freetown. **SLOVENIA:** pp 22, SI-1241 Kamnik. **SOLOMON ISLANDS:** PO Box 166, Honiara. **SOUTH AFRICA:** Private Bag X2067, Krugersdorp, 1740. **SPAIN:** Apartado 132, 28850 Torrejón de Ardoz (Madrid). **SRI LANKA:** 711 Station Road, Wattala 11300. **SURINAME:** PO Box 2914, Paramaribo. **TAHITI, FRENCH POLYNESIA:** BP 7715, 98719 Taravao. **TAIWAN:** No. 325 Shefu Road, Xinwu District, Taoyuan City 32746. **THAILAND:** PO Box 7 Klongchan, Bangkok 10 240. **TRINIDAD AND TOBAGO:** Lower Rapsey Street & Laxmi Lane, Curepe. **TURKEY:** PO Box 23, Feriköy, 34378 İstanbul. **UGANDA:** PO Box 4019, Kampala. **UKRAINE:** PO Box 955, 79491 Lviv - Briukhovychi. **UNITED STATES OF AMERICA:** 25 Columbia Heights, Brooklyn, NY 11201-2483. **VENEZUELA:** Apartado 20.364, Caracas, DC 1020A. **ZAMBIA:** PO Box 33459, 10101 Lusaka. **ZIMBABWE:** Private Bag WG-5001, Westgate. **www.jw.org**